HEBDEN BRIDGE

# Hebden Bridge

*A Sense of Belonging*

Paul Barker

**F**

FRANCES LINCOLN LIMITED
PUBLISHERS

*Frontispiece: The classic Hebden Bridge view – a pen-and-ink postcard design. The stone packhorse bridge over the river Hebden is more than 500 years old. In the 1970s, the mill chimney beyond the bridge was saved from demolition. Originally, it was a manorial corn mill, driven by water power.*

*Endpapers: In a geological bedrock survey, Hebden Bridge lies in the middle of a tract of millstone grit (shown in beige). This hard sandstone stomps up through the middle of the Pennines. To east and west it slices off the coal measures (dark grey) of West Yorkshire and South Lancashire. North and south it butts into the limestone (blue and yellow) of the Yorkshire Dales and the Peak District.*

*Map (pages 16–17): Industrial Hebden Bridge, 1907, at the height of Edwardian prosperity. The general layout hasn't changed much.*

FOR SALLY

Frances Lincoln Ltd
4 Torriano Mews
Torriano Avenue
London NW5 2RZ
www.franceslincoln.com

*Hebden Bridge: A Sense of Belonging*
Copyright © Paul Barker 2012
Illustrations © as listed on page 197

First Frances Lincoln edition 2012

British Library Cataloguing in Publication data
A catalogue record for this book is
available from the British Library

ISBN 978-0-7112-3215-0

9 8 7 6 5 4 3 2 1

# CONTENTS

# LIST OF ILLUSTRATIONS

Frontispiece:  Bridge and mill, p. 2
Map:  Hebden Bridge 1907, pp 16–17

*Picture album between pages 64 and 65*
1. A wedding
2. Mill fire
3. Fleapit
4. Seesaw
5. Sewing shop
6. Hebden Bridge, 1890s
7. Suffragettes
8. Railway station, 1845

*Album between pages 128 and 129*
9. Up Crimsworth
10. Self-help
11 & 12. Puppetry
13 & 14. So Hebden Bridge
15. Industry and art
16. Blanket worker
17. High tea
18. Hippie days
19. Harvest festival
20. Ted Hughes country

Endpapers : Millstone grit

# UNFOLDING THE MAP

In the beginning was the landscape. The narrow Pennine valley of the upper stretches of the river Calder and its cascading tributaries, and the moorland up above. It was, to begin with, a harsh place in which to make a living. Just to get by demanded hard grind and hard graft. The highest praise was 'he's a good worker' or, increasingly, '*she's* a good worker'.

Building on the old skills of handloom weaving, the Industrial Revolution brought to Hebden Bridge and its surrounding villages not only the mills that made cloth but the sewing factories that went on to turn the cloth into cheap ready-made clothing. In the mills, the spinning frames and the looms were sometimes operated by women, but the rows of Singer sewing machines *always* were. The income gave women more independence than in many other places.

Annie Whitaker had worked for fifty-three years in one of the biggest Hebden Bridge sewing shops. When she got her long-service reward – £1 for every year – she thanked the boss, but told him, 'Richard, I think we've got as much right to this firm as you have.' This was where my mother worked as a young woman. She got out as soon as she could. But sometimes, during my childhood, when we were short of money, she would set up the Singer at home and treadle away at out-work. Unused for years, the same machine, with its black-painted iron frame, is now in our spare room.

The present book is an exploration. I have always been intrigued by what it means to talk of the 'sense of place'. At the heart of this isn't just the buildings, however beautiful or bizarre they may be. The point is the people who lived there once, and live there now. A place is not an art object, crafted into some sort of perfection. It is a palimpsest, forever overlaid and underlaid. It has to be scrubbed away at, to get the sense of it.

This is what I try to do here with 'Hebden', the word I use for a tight little cluster of villages and hamlets in the upper Calder valley, not just the large village (or small town) of Hebden Bridge itself. All are now a rather rebellious part of the Calderdale metropolitan borough, which is based in Halifax. Like all villages, these were (and are) great rivals with their neighbours. In the good old days, Hebden Bridge, Mytholmroyd, Heptonstall and the rest had kicking matches against one another, which was a serious business in iron-shod clogs. But they also had a lot in common, though they might deny it. And even more in common now, after all the changes of the last half-century.

Hebden is 'my' place. The place I have the sharpest sense of belonging to. I spent the first eighteen years of my life here. For the first fifteen of those years, I never travelled outside the three counties of the West Riding of Yorkshire, Lancashire and Westmorland. Most of the time, in fact, I never strayed beyond the bounds of the West Riding. As then delineated – from Sedbergh in the far north to Sheffield in the far south – this could boast, and often did, of being the largest county in England.

The Hebden I grew up in was in one of the more obscure corners of the West Riding, tucked away at the Pennine end of the Calder valley, halfway between Halifax and the Lancashire border. Very few people had ever heard of it. For simplicity, I might sometimes say that I came from the 'Brontë end' of Yorkshire, which was, I reckoned, fairly clear. The supposed site of Wuthering Heights was only a Sunday afternoon's walk away.

Given this isolation, the Hebden of my childhood and adolescence was very self-contained, even self-obsessed. Like many of my contemporaries, I left and was glad to leave.

An anecdote. After graduation, and a year's university teaching abroad, I at last got a proper London job. So I looked in on the manager of the Hebden Bridge branch of Lloyds, in its fine stone-built premises at the corner of Albert Street. It was the sort of thing you did in those days. The point was to thank him for letting me run up an overdraft when I was almost income-less.

I said 'I'm glad to say I've got a job on *The Times*.' He smiled and said 'Oh, that's nice. I look forward to seeing you around the village.' The local paper was, and is, the *Hebden Bridge Times* (usually called, simply, the *Bridge Times*). On beginning this book, I renewed my subscription.

In Hebden Bridge, and its neighbouring village of Mytholmroyd, I often felt to be related to about a third of the place. My mother and father had lived here all their lives. Their roots went back many generations. Nearly all the surnames – Barker, Greenwood, Sutcliffe, Ashworth, Thomas – that you found in family histories, and sometimes in family bibles, were as local as the millstone-grit sandstone that almost all the houses and farms were built out of. The gloriously coloured maps of the British Bedrock Geology Survey show Hebden sitting on a narrow strip of millstone grit: independent of the Lancashire and Yorkshire coal strata on either side, and south of the limestone of the Dales. I sometimes think the obdurate, utilitarian nature of that rock tells you all you need to know about the psychology of old Hebden.

The story of each Hebden family usually began on the hilltops, with subsistence farming, and ended in the valley, in a textile mill. To me, this network of people and experiences is central to what a sense of place means. I think that the same would be true of many other towns and villages. But Hebden is perhaps a specially vivid example.

My wife, Sally, is also local and, like me, she left. But we kept coming back – with four children, eventually – to see parents, relatives and friends. On overseas holidays, we would sometimes be asked: 'Where are you from?' The answer was: 'We live in London but we're from Yorkshire, really.' Our Yorkshire is this strip of about 5 miles along the upper valley of the Calder, with even narrower side-valleys that may wind for miles up into the hills. I am pursuing the sense of place – this sense of belonging – with a microscope. My own biography and Hebden's intertwine.

My primary school, in Mytholmroyd, was the one my father and my grandfather had been at. They left early to go into a mill. My mother went straight into the sewing shop from her own Hebden Bridge school.

For both of my parents, in the end, shop-keeping gave them the way out into a better life – and a more independent one. Hebden was, and is, a non-deferential place. No one was called 'Sir'.

When the factories and sewing shops collapsed – a process that began early in the twentieth century and culminated in the 1960s and 1970s, a new era began. If I make use of a Lloyds Bank cheque – now an increasingly rare event, of course – it states that Hebden Bridge is my home branch. I no longer have to explain where the place is. Almost everyone in Britain either seems to have been there or knows someone who has. Tourism, reportage, the arts (including the link with the Poet Laureate Ted Hughes, who was born in Mytholmroyd): all have brought much greater prominence, but not always greater happiness.

My own map of Hebden, in this book, is a triangulation of personal memoir, direct observation and social history. I have done a great deal of delving, at various times, into the historical record. But I have tried to present a narrative, rather than a heaped-up window display of background research.

Some years ago, when I was beginning to think about all this, I undertook a series of interviews with people who lived locally. Many of them were old enough to have memories that stretched far back into the early years of the twentieth century. They also remembered stories they were told by fathers, mothers, uncles and aunts. As everyone knows, memory is tricky. Over the years, it can be reshaped into a narrative which isn't the way things actually were. But the reshaping tells a story in its own right.

I draw on these interviews here. They took place in the late 1970s; mostly in 1978. In Hebden, at that time, change was everywhere in the air. Newcomers were arriving in large numbers. There was both new conflict and new hope. In 2010–11, I went back, specifically in order to see how these changes had worked out. Had the place become reunited, with locals and newcomers all reconciled and homogenised, like a carton of long-life milk? And how did the one-time newcomers feel about a new wave of arrivals?

Nothing stands still. There will, no doubt, be further change after I've completed this book. Where I focus directly on the older interviews, I try to make this doubly clear by a consistent use of the past tense. With interviews from 2010–11, I use the present tense. So, for example, Jonas and Vera Brown, and William Sutcliffe (chapters headed 'Fire' and 'Lady Willie') were interviewed in 1978; Chris Ratcliffe and Mike Barrett ('Family') were interviewed in 2010.

Hebden is a very special place. Some may think that, in its aching trendiness, it's away with the fairies. For others, it's somewhere over the rainbow. This book may be a triangulation, but it is also – and perhaps more importantly – a quest and a celebration.

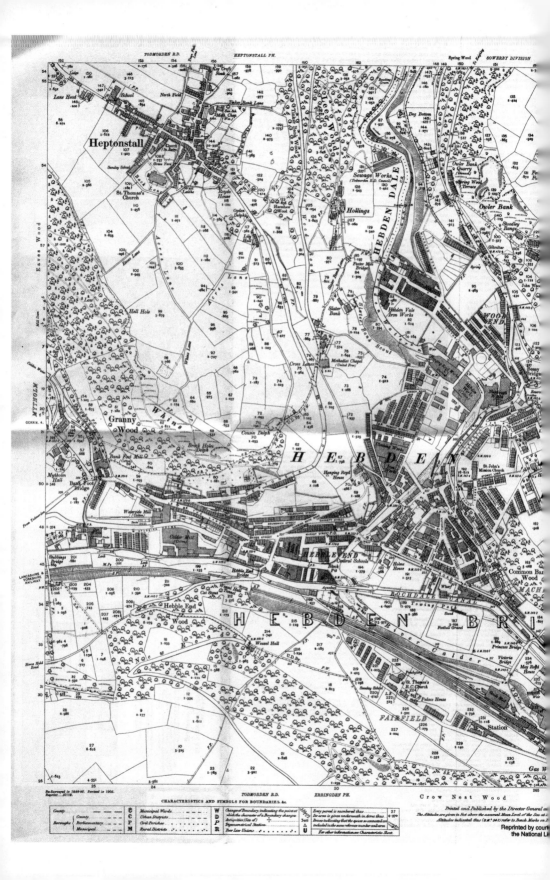

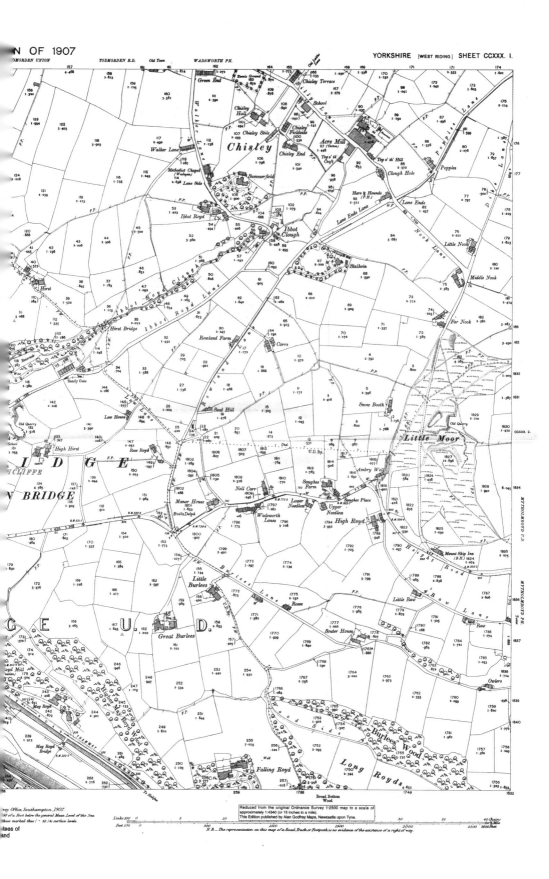

Green End

Chisley Terrace

Chisley School

Acre Mill

Chisley Hall

Chisley Stile

Chisley Fieldside

Chisley End

Chisley

Walker Lane

Top o' th' Hill

Top o' th' Croft

Clough Hole

Popples

Methodist Chapel (Wesleyan)

Lane Side

Sumnerfield

Hare & Hounds (P.H.)

Lane Ends

Ibbot Royd

Ibbot Clough

Lane Ends Lane

Stalheim

Little Nook

Middle Nook

Hirst

Far Nook

Hirst Bridge

Rowland Farm

Carrs

Reservoir

Sandy Gate

Seed Hill

Snow Booth

Little Moor

Old Quarry

High Hirst

Law House

Raw Royd

Little Moor

Ambry Well

CCXXX. 2.

I D G E

CLIFFE

N BRIDGE

Manor House

Butts Delph

Nell Carr

Wadsworth Lanes

Lower Noodles

Upper Noodles

Saughes Farm

Saughes Place

High Royd

Height Road

Mount Skip Inn (B.H.)

Little Burlees

Burlees Lane

Rosse

Little Raw

Raw

G E    U  D.

Great Burlees

Souter House

Owlers

Royd Mill

May Royd

May Royd Bridge

Falling Royd

Burlees Wood

Long Royds

Broad Bottom Wood

TRAMWAY

METHROYD U.D.

METHROYD PH.

Reduced from the original Ordnance Survey 1:2500 map to a scale of
approximately 1:4340 (or 15 inches to a mile)
This Edition published by Alan Godfrey Maps, Newcastle upon Tyne.

N.B.— The representation on this map of a Road, Track or Footpath is no evidence of the existence of a right of way

Links 100    0    5    10    20    30    40 Chains
Feet 100    0    500    1000    2000    2500    3600 Feet

# I. BRASS

A young woman is playing a trombone in a street band at a Bradford mayoral ceremony. People, it seems, have been instructed to be cheerful in spite of the sneaky West Yorkshire wind. Even now, for a woman, a trombone is an unusual choice of instrument. I wander over to the fringe of the band, and ask her where she is based. 'Hebden Bridge,' she says. 'Where else could it be?' She is an 'offcomer', one of the outsiders who have moved into this Pennine small town and its surrounding villages and hamlets.

Her own windswept hamlet, once seen locally as 'the back of beyond', is now two-thirds 'professional and managerial', according to the census. The hilltop school, once threatened with closure, is now overflowing with children. But the trombonist has become a true Brigger – as the natives always used to call themselves – with that characteristic stubborn resilience.

Here is Dick Straightup, in Ted Hughes's poem of that name, from his 1960 collection, *Lupercal*, dedicated to his then wife Sylvia Plath:

> Past eighty, but never in eighty years -
> Eighty winters on the windy ridge
> Of England – has he buttoned his shirt or his jacket.
> He sits in the bar-room seat he has been
> Polishing with his backside sixty-odd years
> Where nobody else sits.

Dick Straightup was a real person, Hughes's uncle. Hughes reports that he 'banged the big bass drum' in the village band. From the early years of my life in Hebden (where Hughes spent his own childhood), I half-remember Dick Straightup. Or is what I remember my father talking about him? The pub Hughes writes about is in the middle of the hill village of Heptonstall, overlooking Hebden. Sylvia Plath, who killed herself in London in 1963, is buried in the graveyard of Heptonstall church, among the local dead.

Hebden Bridge has made the transit from the Yorkshire Pennines' traditional economy of textiles-plus-farming to a town – many would call it a large village – that now thrives as a home for arts and crafts. That is, something much more than a dormitory for nearby cities. In a sequence of British cities, beginning in London, many districts have been 'gentri-fied' in recent decades. That is, they've gone from being almost wholly working class enclaves to becoming mostly middle class. In London, this social shift began in Islington and Camden Town in the 1940s and 1950s. It was a kind of would-be kindly colonisation. The same process has now spread to the countryside. Some geographers call it 'greentrifica-tion' – meaning rural gentrification, One academic study, published in 2002, takes Hebden Bridge, from the 1970s on, as a prime example of this social change. The alternative, at the time, was disastrous decline. The population had fallen to half what it had been fifty years before.

Other towns or villages have tried to pull off the same transition to a new prosperity. Hay-on-Wye in the Welsh borders, is one success story, thanks to two men: a second-hand bookseller, Richard Booth, and a festival organiser, Peter Florence. Totnes in Devon and Stroud in Gloucestershire both have some affinity with Hebden. Many other towns have failed. But Hebden succeeded. Luck may have played its part, as when Hughes emerged as one of the major English poets of his day. Now you have Poet Laureate tours, led by a retired rag-trade cutter and amateur watercolourist.

But more important than luck was the local high percentage of energy and adaptability.

The transition didn't happen without conflict. Between offcomers, who delighted in the idea of a 'community', and the established (though dwindling) community itself. There were battles between squatters and the advocates of demolishing supposedly outdated housing (all of it now happily lived in). As Hebden becomes much more like a 'normal' place, with the accompanying class divides, a third conflict has grown up, between the original set of offcomers – leftist, arty-crafty, New Agey – and those for whom Hebden is just a pleasant place to commute from.

I never went back to live there full time after leaving school. Most of the people I took A-levels with, left, and never returned. Not that there were many of them. The classes in which I studied for A-levels never held more than half a dozen; for Latin I was in a class of two.

Hebden Bridge was then a little-known mill town, though for social historians it had an honoured place in the annals of industry. One textile factory, Nutclough mill, which opened in 1873, was singled out by the socialist historians, Beatrice and Sidney Webb, as an almost unique example, in Britain, of a successful worker cooperative. Profits were shared. It ran until 1918, then went bust. To save jobs, the factory was taken over by the central Cooperative Wholesale Society in Manchester. Thereafter it was run like any other business – though, by the time I could see it from my teenage bedroom window, with less and less success.

My school badge bore gilt-embroidered smoking mill chimneys. Implicit (or explicit) message: 'Where there's muck there's brass.' The local Little Theatre, for amateur actors, founded in 1924 and still flourishing, acquired an Art Deco logo which showed a female figure – perhaps the muse of drama – against a celebratory background of the Hebden Bridge old packhorse bridge and smoky mill chimneys. The theme was 'the Arts rising from Industry'.

When one of the upstream dye works had a busy day, the river ran blue. But when the mill smoke cleared from over the valley, you could see the surrounding hillside beauty.

Now Hebden, with its environs, is, some say, the lesbian capital of Britain. Certainly, the streetscape always includes an unusually high proportion of women couples. Instead of manufacturing cloth for cheap trousers, Hebden started to manufacture lifestyles. When I went back for a stream-side family picnic in the late 1970s, we found ourselves snapped by the young Martin Parr, fresh out of his Manchester art school, for his 'local customs' files. The photographer was one of the earliest offcomers.

What made Hebden what it was, and what it now is? Geography? History? Psychology? Stir all three ingredients together and you begin to get some feel for a place not quite like any other. Brass, fiddle and harp perhaps. Such rich music.

Geographically, you could begin by climbing up the steep road at the end of Market Street, past a Co-op supermarket and the former Lord Nelson pub, and across the humpbacked stone bridge over the Rochdale canal. The road goes up to Horsehold, an oddly named spur of rock, below which the hillside falls away sharply.

On the way up, you've gone past Weasel Hall, an old farmhouse where, as a child, I was sometimes taken to visit my great-uncle Ira Greenwood. The original Ira was King David's priest. After the Reformation, his name became a favourite among Protestants, especially Nonconformists. At Weasel Hall, the chief fascination was to watch the 'bees' rising and falling in the tall glass jar of Balm of Gilead on his mantelpiece. The bees were poplar buds, left in the water to ferment. The outcome was a sweet drink, which had traces of an aspirin-like chemical. It was said to be good for sore throats and coughs.

At the top of Horsehold, you look out across the upper Calder valley where two small tributaries join the Calder: the Colden and the Hebden. Between the two, at the top of another steep hill, you see Dick Straightup's Heptonstall. For centuries, when the riverside below was marshy and generally unappealing, Heptonstall was the main settlement hereabouts. The bridge over the Hebden (Hepton Bridge) was simply the quickest way up for the packhorse men. They brought in wool for uplands families to weave at home, and picked up the lengths of woven cloth for sale in Halifax's eighteenth-century Piece Hall market.

The flat land around the Calder is a narrow ribbon at this point in the river's journey from its source, just over the Lancashire border, down to its junction with the river Aire. From there, the water from the moors eventually outpours into the Humber and the North Sea. Any fairly level land in Hebden Bridge and Mytholmroyd – where the valley opens out a bit – was prime land to build on, once the Leeds–Manchester railway arrived in the 1840s and mill masters began to shift jobs from water power to steam, and from wool to cotton. Most of the side-valley mills, where streams ran fast enough to turn water-wheels, were abandoned. Some of them had been notorious for the death rate of the orphan and workhouse children. As townships, Hebden and Mytholmroyd became a kind of twin star. Each revolved around the other, with many of the mills owned by the same families. But each, also, saw the other place as a competitor.

From Horsehold, you see the hilltops bare and clad with heather. If the heather is in bloom, the moors look like a calendar picture. Otherwise, you need a taste for a special kind of bleakness. This is why I like East Anglia almost as much as the Pennines: both are landscapes that don't pander to you. On such days, the moorland is enlivened only by the clouds scudding above it. Unfortunately, the Pennines have never had a John Constable to celebrate their cloudscape.

Below the moors, your eye can easily pick out the 'spring line', where streams emerged from under the moorland. This line is marked by the oldest farms and by hamlets with names like Old Town, Pecket Well and Midgley. Here are the fields which were just broad enough for subsistence farming. Some sheep, some dairy cows, some wheat and barley. Below them, the land falls away again, through broadleaf woodland, down to the riverside.

Except at Hebden Bridge itself. Staring across the valley, you can see that great ingenuity was used to build houses on the steep slopes. They are what give the place its characteristic look. The houses are stone terraces, four storeys high. The terraces were mostly built around the end of the nineteenth century, when the prosperity of (old-style) Hebden was at its height. This good fortune sprang from the emergent mass-consumption among a working class whose wages were at last benefiting from a Victorian economic boom. The special Hebden line was weaving and dyeing fustian and corduroy cloth, then making this cloth up into trousers. Fustian is a smooth, tough fabric made by slicing along the ridges of corduroy – originally, knife in hand – and opening the cloth out flat. Hebden Bridge became known as Fustianopolis.

The trick of the tall terraces is this. The two upper storeys of the houses are built as one dwelling, with a door entered from a street along the back. The lower two storeys are a separate dwelling, entered from a street along the front. (Sometimes the division is three storeys above, and one below.) The under-houses were cheaper because they were wholly, or mainly, 'back to earth'. It was impossible to keep the damp out.

My mother's father ran a small shuttle factory. He died in the 1919 Spanish flu epidemic. His widow and children were pushed down towards the poverty line. The family moved to one of these lower terrace houses. Symbolically, the widow, my maternal grandmother, kept the piano. She herself went into one of the many local sewing shops – the rag-trade factories – to work. So did her elder daughter, who had previously worked in her father's office. When the younger daughter, my mother, passed the exam for a free place at the grammar school, she couldn't take it up because my grandmother could not guarantee to keep her at school beyond the statutory leaving age. If you agreed but then reneged, you had to pay back the scholarship money. At fourteen, my mother also went into a sewing shop.

In Hebden, making a living was a joint family enterprise. Most women undertook paid work, as well as men. In this, Hebden was ahead of its time. Historically, this quest for work is one reason why this corner of the Pennines was a wellspring of the Industrial Revolution. People who have it easy don't innovate. You had to find some way to add to your earnings.

One early way, in this usefully out-of-the-way place, was coining. You clipped gold or silver from the edge of coins, melted the stolen metal, and made your home-made versions. In the late seventeenth century, the Royal Mint introduced milled edges to try to put an end to this, without any immediate success. The Mint also tried to end the chronic shortage of state coinage. Portuguese moidores and Spanish pieces of eight had circulated in England to make up the shortfall. And the more diverse the designs of coins are, the easier it is to fool the public. Calder valley coiners saw the moidore as the easiest money to fake.

One of the most notorious coiners, David Hartley, called King David, operated in and around Mytholmroyd. He was hanged at York in 1770. His body was brought back to Heptonstall churchyard for burial. If the light is right, I can just make out his name among the black grave-slabs. He came home at the end.

Long-term, handloom weaving was a better alternative. It was steadier work, and didn't attract the eyes of the excisemen. The husband minded the sheep on the small farm. The wife and her mother spun the yarn. Some of the wool was from their own sheep, the rest was brought in by the packmen. Husband and wife both wove it. The children, of whatever age, helped with everything.

These were the people that John and Charles Wesley, and their preacher followers, tried to bring back to a more direct form of Christian belief than was offered by the somnolent Anglican church. At Heptonstall, a unique octagonal Methodist chapel marks where John Wesley came to his hilltop meetings.

For his classic history, *The Making of the English Working Class*, E.P. Thompson, then a Leeds university lecturer living in nearby Halifax, gathered much of his best material from the upper Calder valley. In one ferocious chapter, he accused the Methodists of seducing the workers away from becoming true revolutionaries. Half a century after he wrote this, several crashed or drastically retooled leftist revolutions – Russia, China, Cambodia, Cuba, Nicaragua, to name but five – make this seem like a less plausible accusation. But Methodism and its offshoots permanently marked the place. In and around Hebden, when I grew up there, I counted almost twenty chapels and churches. Most have gone: adapted for other uses or demolished. The demolished chapels include the two I went to as a child and in my early teens. (I mainly went for the benefit of the book prizes for good attendance.) But the chapels' frugal, self-help spirit lives on.

And the psychology? In the second chapter of Mrs Gaskell's *Life of Charlotte Brontë*, she tries to pin down the characteristics of the Yorkshire Pennine people. The analysis was, and is, instantly recognisable by anyone who grew up in Hebden. The Brontës' Haworth is just across the moors. The Gaskell description would be acknowledged by local people, with some smugness:

Even an inhabitant of the neighbouring county of Lancaster is struck by the peculiar force of character which the Yorkshiremen display. This makes them interesting as a race; while, at the same time, as individuals, the remarkable degree of self-sufficiency they possess gives them an air of independence rather apt to repel a stranger.

Yes, that's it, they would say in Hebden. Nutclough mill – cotton spinning, weaving, dyeing – may have been, for a few years, among the very few workers' cooperatives that ever made the economic grade. But life was not all sweetness and light. I think of an ageing brother and sister

I spoke to in a bare, stone-floor farmhouse at the top of a small valley. They would spend their winters snowed in.

Surprisingly, my Hebden Bridge branch of Lloyds bank is still there – though nearly all the business is now handled at Halifax, seven miles away, or by telephone, or on the internet. The *Hebden Bridge Times* is also still there, but its offices are no longer in a converted chapel with a sundial and tomb-stones (this is now a bric-a-brac shop). The business side is run from Leeds.

The close-knit web of local surnames has dwindled. Once you couldn't go far down the street without meeting a Greenwood, Sutcliffe, Pickles, Ingham, Whitaker or Uttley. My mother and my wife's mother, though apparently unrelated, were both *née* Marion Ashworth. There was even a fair sprinkling of Barkers. This name comes from the men who stripped bark off trees for the tanning of leather. The trade carried on, in some places, into the twentieth century.

'Barker' is a fairly general north country tag. But some of the Hebden names were very local indeed. You can assume that the family of anyone, anywhere, called Greenwood comes ultimately from Hebden Bridge and environs; anyone called Sutcliffe has family origins in Halifax. As in Wales (whence Dylan Thomas's Organ Morgan, Butcher Beynon and Evans the Death in his play, *Under Milk Wood*), so in Hebden: by-names were used as a way of telling apart families with identical surnames, and often first names also: Tom o'Harry's, Johnny Ninepence ('because he was thruppence short of a shilling'), Lady Willie. Dick Straightup had been christened Richard Uttley. In Hebden there were so many Greenwoods and Sutcliffes, especially, that no one never would knew whom you were talking about, without the by-name.

All this has changed. Among the ninety-nine students listed in the summer 2011 A-level results at the local comprehensive, Calder High School, those old surnames hardly featured. One Greenwood; one Sutcliffe. The names Ingham, Cockcroft, Shackleton and Barker also cropped up only once. The rest nowhere. No Ashworth, no Whitaker, no Farrar, no Thomas.

The population had been falling since the 1901 census. Competitors muscled in. Many of the local textile firms linked up, fairly loosely, in the ominous-sounding 'Combine'. It was a semi-secret business, a cartel. The Combine's member-firms kept their own names and mills, and their own counsel.

Hebden went on to ride the traumas of the 1930s slump fairly well – because there was a spread of work: cotton, with the local specialism in fustian and corduroy, and the sewing shops to go with this; some silk and wool; light engineering; day-old chicks; small-scale farming. The contrast people always made – like Mrs Gaskell – was with Lancashire, just across the county border.

The ups and downs of the intensive cotton-spinning monoculture created a very different way of life (finely described in the Blackburn-born historian William Woodruff's autobiography, *The Road to Nab End*). Hebden always felt a cut above the Lancashire catch-as-catch-can style. Border settlements always try hardest to claim they are different from those on the other side. Herefordshire tries very hard to assert its non-Welshness, Alsace tries to shed its Germanness. Ditto Hebden, even though the local dialect included both Yorkshire and Lancashire words.

The Second World War is often cited as a force for social change. Here, by contrast, it may have held back change. A kind of historical weir. The ethic of self-help was held on to. Children still played the old-style games. (I was proud, later on, to help the folklorists, Peter and Iona Opie, enter 'dobber' into their files, for an especially large marble.) The power of locality was strengthened, not weakened. The great conflict was a strange, distant war. The bombers flew over to destroy the docks of Liverpool or Manchester. A single bomb fell on Halifax. (The bomb site is now a little Peace Park, in a neighbourhood that is predominantly Kashmiri.) That was it.

From the 1950s, the weir started to crumble. In the late 1960s, it gave way. The textile businesses collapsed: the spinning, the weaving, the dyeing, the sewing shops for the ready-made trade. Nearly all of them went. It was partly due to cheaper goods from abroad. Partly it was due to the then Labour government's obsession with bringing small textile firms together into larger conglomerates. The notorious, and often elusive, 'economic efficiencies of scale'.

Hebden's ready-mades were never at the top end of the market. Contracts with British Home Stores, not Marks & Spencer, kept the sewing shops in business. In fact, in Hebden, there was deep suspicion of the close control M&S inflicted on their suppliers. 'They get you making everything to their specification,' I was told. 'Really, they're running the firm. Then they drop the contract, and you're sunk.' Monopoly capitalism has often been written about. The way M&S worked was a textbook example of *monopsony* – the great power of a sole buyer. In Hebden, firms preferred to run their own show for as long as they could.

When foreign competition re-established itself, from the 1950s, it took a form that exposed Hebden's inward-looking habits. Jeans began to take over the market for cheap trousers. They were nearly all made abroad. Hebden didn't believe the fashion would last. Firms were set in their ways. Jeans went on to conquer Hebden's old market. It was the end of a story. Almost the only firm that survived, for a while, was a Mytholmroyd company that made jodhpurs.

Hebden had always been a predominantly working class place. There was a light sprinkling of doctors, head teachers, solicitors, bank managers and the like. But there was no very visible *rentier* class. There were few, if any, people who had incomes from un-obvious sources. The feel was very different from that of a similar-sized large village or small town in, say, Sussex or Wiltshire. I'm used to this now, but it came as a shock when I first went to London. So did the notably taller and better-fed people in the streets.

But now, in Hebden, an air of decline started to settle very quickly. Houses fell empty. Shops closed. The local planners, aided and abetted by the local health officialdom, thought that the answer was demolition – maybe even 40 per cent of the older houses in Hebden Bridge – and a new road driven through the middle of town. This was halted by an early conservation movement. Headed by an old friend of mine – one A-level student who did return after graduation – the conservationists even won a political majority on the district council. An early Green triumph. From the 1970s, regeneration began.

Squatters moved into the empty houses (defying the local hostility). The word got around among art students or recent art graduates. Ill-paid lecturers at Manchester, Leeds or Huddersfield polytechnics followed. When Granada TV was a Manchester-based cultural force, Heptonstall – once noted for its inbred curmudgeonliness – became known as Granada Village; so many of the staff had settled there. Those BBC staff who have relocated to Manchester will follow a similar trail.

With two poet friends, Ted Hughes had helped to open the first Arvon creative writing centre in north Devon in 1968. Soon afterwards Arvon started up a northern branch in a former mill-master's house, called Lumb Bank, on the hills above Hebden Bridge. As more and more people came to Arvon, to learn or to teach, and to enjoy the local pubs (including Dick Straightup's favourite), they saw what an attractive place it was. The word spread further.

The artiness has never faded. It has put its own indelible mark on Hebden. As I write this, there are three bookshops. In my childhood there wasn't even one.

This remains brass band country. With little success, I briefly tried to play cornet in the Hebden Bridge band. This band still exists and plays carols in the square in the middle of town at Christmas. In competitions it pits itself against the very best. The 1996 film, *Brassed Off*, starring Peter Postlethwaite and Jim Carter, movingly evokes this continuing Yorkshire obsession. Typically, the film's lament is much less sentimental than the Durham-based *Billy Elliott*, with which it is often compared. As the *Oxford Dictionary of Music* confirms, the Mortimer family of Hebden Bridge – Fred, Harry, Alex, Rex – were among the northern band movement's leaders. When Harry's son visited Hebden Bridge in 2011, the *Hebden Bridge Times* hailed him as 'brass band royalty'.

From coiners' refuge, through hive of industry, to 'Greenwich Village of the North' (a description coined by the novelist and Arvon tutor Angela Carter), there's no doubt that Hebden continues to make a music of its own. But is it all harmony?

# 2. FIRE

My first memory is of being taken to see Olympia on fire. I was about three. The grand name designated a red-brick weaving shed at Mytholmroyd. It was on one side of the canal. We watchers – men, women and children – all stood on the other side, on the 'cut bank'. The *cut* was the Rochdale canal, the *bank* was the towpath. Serious traffic along the waterway had ceased years ago, but you still saw, sometimes, cutters or dredgers clearing the reeds and the mud. No one foresaw, then, that narrowboats would become a hobby, even a way of life; that all the cumbersome wooden locks would be repaired; and that, long after Olympia mill had gone, the canal would flourish again.

Fires were a form of free public entertainment. There were plenty of mills, so there were plenty of fires. Sometimes these were genuine accidents. Always there was the suspicion that it was a way for a failing firm to get rid of the buildings and claim the insurance. I never remember anyone being prosecuted. The slander remained at the level of gossip, a knowing smile and a tap on the side of the nose, in pubs, chapels or bowling clubs. Ill-stored cotton waste, and wooden floors sodden with lubrication oil from the looms, made wonderful fuel. The mills went up like a Fifth of November bonfire, though without the sparklers and bangers.

I have loved fires all my life, ever since. I think the fascination began on that chilly evening, watching Olympia go down. The way to the fire was cold – we lived on the other side of the village – but when you got there you could feel the heat blazing out right across the water. The fire brigades from Mytholmroyd and Hebden Bridge – one fire brigade each – had driven up across the little stone bridge across the canal. I doubt if they had much hope of stopping the fire. The job was to stop it spreading. Just along from the bridge was the Mytholmroyd gasometer – no one except pedants ever called such things 'gas holders' – built by the local, pre-nationalisation, coal-fired gas works to keep up the pressure in the mains. More important to me, a wooden door between the gasometer and the canal led into my grandfather's 'hen pen' – his chicken huts – where I would sometimes go and put handfuls of Indian corn into the feeder trays of the battery hens, to encourage them to lay eggs with yellower yolks. No one that I came across ever saw any harm in keeping hens caged, and it was years before I heard anyone call the corn 'maize'.

There was one drawback of being so near to the canal. Rats. The long body of one rat, caught in a rat trap, was nailed up on a hut wall. The idea was to deter the others. I don't know if it worked. But just as I date my love of fires from the crackle and collapse of Olympia mill, so I date my loathing of rats from that rat on the wall. Years later, the first novel I ever read straight through, well into the night, was *1984*. I'd borrowed it from one of the county council's local branch libraries (to which I owed much of my education). I went to bed at about two, completely sympathising with Winston Smith about the horror of getting close to rats. I still feel the same.

Unlike many of the mills which burned down, Olympia was rebuilt. When I went with my tape recorder to see Jonas Brown in the late 1970s, he lived at the end house in a terrace near the canal, opposite Olympia. He'd gone straight from school to work at Olympia. The boss was Jim Mitchell. 'He were just an ordinary working man who'd moved from cutting fustians with a razor blade.' Jonas had the usual local reluctance to be subservient to bosses.

'There was 500 gallons of diesel oil down in the bottom,' Jonas said, 'and didn't it burn! The donkey engine backfired and up it went. We shouted to all the women workers "Get out, get out, or you'll be burned alive." One or two worried about stopping the frames and all that carry-on. They were told "Just get out".'

Jonas was very self-contained, as I talked to him. His style was slightly aggressive. 'Olympia was just old looms picked up cheap. If there was a night-time breakdown, there were no spares. We'd wait to go to Fleetwood's, blacksmiths, in the morning. I can see old Fleetwood now, a little fat chap with a leather apron. They did a lot of welding.'

I sometimes looked in at the smithy, by then run by Fleetwood's son Herbert, on my way back from school. He shod farm horses. The best moment was when he put the red-hot iron to sizzle in the water. The only horses in the valley then were the few that remained on farms and one or two belonging to general carriers, each with their own horse and cart. Enough to move the little furniture most people had. One Mytholmroyd carrier had trained his horse to bring him back home drunk from the pub, without any guidance.

After the fire, Jonas was only out of work for five or six weeks. 'I took the dole only once in my life. They didn't give it to you, they threw it at you. I did a bit of haymaking and other jobs. I even traded in old shotguns, buying them and then posting them on to a Manchester repair firm.' After new looms were put in, he went back to Olympia.

He learnt to jacquard-weave. 'There were four German Jews, showing us how to do it. On the sixteen-shaft jacquards, weaving silk, you were paid by the yard. The night shift was seven at night till six in t'morning. That were the good old days.'

Jacquard looms – one of the forerunners of computer programming – were preset to weave elaborate patterns. 'We wove cloth for curtains. I wove the altar cloth for St Michael's church, Mytholmroyd. I always enjoyed weaving. You can always learn. I wove beautiful things for King Haakon of Norway and Queen Wilhelmina of Holland. Damask. But silk was worse-paid than cotton.' He eventually 'got a bit fed up' and moved to Ronnie Stell's nearby cotton mill: 'Corduroys, moles, twills, jeans. Ronnie was a good boss. Too good in a way. Wasn't stern enough. I watch fourteen looms now, one when I started. It's automation. But you've got to have your warp and you've got to have your weft, whatever you do.

'We were all struggling to get on. We were no worse off then, except that working hours are a lot shorter [in the 1970s]. And women are paid the same; it used to be half. If you couldn't afford to go on holiday, you just stayed in Mytholmroyd and looked in at Donnie Barker, if he were open.' Donald Barker was my father. In those days he ran a fish and chip shop by the railway station. 'You might go on to Halifax, to the Palace, to see the variety acts. I saw *Chu Chin Chow* at the Palace.'

At the same music hall I later saw Jasper Maskelyne, the famous magician, and the comedy orchestra, Dr Crock and his Crackpots.

Jonas said he meant to retire in a couple of years, when he got the state pension. 'Enough's enough. From childhood you're told what to do, from schoolmasters on. At sixty-five, if you're lucky to get so far, you can then tell them what to do. It's as simple as that is life, if you think about it seriously.'

The Browns' house was built at the same time as an adjacent works, Westfield mill. The houses nearest to the canal were for managers or foremen. 'There's a lot of fancy work around,' Jonas said, 'like the cornice mouldings and the alabaster rose in the middle of the ceiling.' Across the canal, Olympia has now vanished. 'Courtaulds and other big firms buy the little firms out. Then they close them.' Where Olympia had stood, there is only a strip of grass in front of the seventeenth-century Redacre farm which used to be hidden behind it. As always, it is a surprise to see how big a factory could be built on such a small patch of land.

Westfield mill has also vanished, as if by magic. My father, grand-father and great-grandfather all worked here. My father went to the Burnley Road board school a few hundred yards away, as I did. But whereas I passed the old-time eleven-plus and took up a free place at Hebden Bridge grammar school, he left full-time school at eleven, and worked part-time till thirteen, when his schooling ended. Board school pupils were taught the national anthems of all the first world war allies. He remembered the opening words of the 'Marseillaise' for the rest of his life.

One of Westfield's pair of chimneys had the name 'Westfield' embla-zoned on it in white tiles. Much later, I went to see it felled. I stood on the next canal bridge along, to get a good view. The pleasure of watching demolitions came second only to watching fires.

Jonas Brown was as local in his life and ways as anyone in Hebden. But he wasn't born locally. He'd moved in from Nelson, just over the hills in Lancashire, when he was six. His father was trying to escape the slump. In the first world war, he was killed at Passchendaele. 'He's in a cemetery just outside where the Belgian looms came from.' Jonas grew

up in a hamlet in a Mytholmroyd side-valley, 'where you knew everyone by name: "Hello Donnie, hello George, hello Abie".' George and
Abraham were two of my father's brothers.

His wife Vera worked in the sewing shops but she said that her father
'was out of work for years and years'. Her family was helped by neighbours: 'Second-hand clothes, end of joint, cheap Japanese socks, broken
biscuits.' She disliked the rag trade. 'All the women was afraid of the
bosses. It was "please" and "thank you" and they gave you money as
if they were doing you a favour.' Jonas: 'You're doing *them* a favour,
working for them, if you look at it theoretically.' Oddly, perhaps, Jonas
was no unionist. He described himself as 'half in, half out'. When he
spoke of 'one or two little Hitlers' at the weaving shed, he meant shop
stewards. His creed was individualist.

# 3 . LADY WILLIE

Lady Willie lived in a house on the hillside along from Heptonstall. It had cement lions on the gateposts and a bright green lawn. Some council houses encroached at the back, but the house itself was self-enclosed and dark. This is where William Sutcliffe – to give him the name no one ever called him by – had lived man and boy. He and his brother Harold now ran a restaurant here. A restaurant in the old Hebden sense: specialising in high teas. My mother-in-law used to go there annually for a reunion of the women she'd been at school with. On one visit they thought that the cat on the window seat kept remarkably still. Going across to it, they found out why. The cat was dead.

When I said I was going up, I was told by one regular patron: 'It smells old. But it *is* a bit cheaper than anywhere else.' The telephone at Lady Willie's rang steadily with reservations.

There were books everywhere, even in the dining room. Lady Willie was in a snug little room off the hallway. He sat on an old sofa, holding a black cane with a gold head. There was a cheery coal fire in the grate. Old-fashioned chairs with upholstered seats were tucked into various corners of the room. A pair of trousers and a jacket were on one chair. My main impression was of a book-lined cell. There was a sweetish smell.

Lady Willie looked tired. He had had a bladder operation at the infirmary in Halifax. He was due to go back there soon. He held his neck stiffly and rubbed his side sometimes. But his face became almost convulsed when he laughed. He laughed almost silently. I'd never met him before, and I could see that, if he were well, he would be very camp. Every so often he lifted a finger from the cane, to make a point. Locally he was well known not only for his restaurant but also for his addresses from local pulpits. He loved to tell a tale. He was 'a character' – which was one of the greatest endorsements in Hebden.

Lady Willie moved into this house when he was nine years old. It was a smallholding, running down to the Colden river. His father was a butcher by trade. 'Then he had a brainwave. Let's make teas. Boiled ham, boiled tongue, roasted chickens. On the first day, not a soul turned up. We had to eat it all ourselves. But he wasn't put off.'

The big mill hereabouts was Jack Bridge, on the river Colden. It was surrounded by fields and moor. By the time I was talking to Willie, in the 1970s, almost every trace of it had gone. 'All the chapels have been pulled down – gone – as well. The last one left is the Baptist chapel at Heptonstall Slack, and that's standing empty. Everyone got married at Slack, or buried there. Start or finish at Slack.' (My own mother and my sister Elaine were both married at this hilltop chapel.)

Willie went to Colden school, like everyone else. 'A foregone conclusion. But it was a good school, a good headmistress, a topper. She encouraged you to read.' Like me, Willie collected Sunday school prizes. But, unusually, his family were Anglicans. 'I was the only Anglican at Colden school. There was a lot of hostility. Nothing rough, but I walked the three miles to and from Heptonstall church every Sunday morning without fail. They looked at you as you went past. But generally people didn't notice what Anglicans did. They were all Methodists.

'In Heptonstall there was no work. They all went down Hebden, or stayed at home, looking out of the windows. It got that I wouldn't walk down the high street. All those eyes.'

He left school as soon as he could. 'No money.' But he went to night school. 'I was always an avid reader. They used to *call* me [tell me off]. Always your nose is in a book. Get some work done. For that generation, work was the be-all and end-all. A man could thrash his wife, turn her out, come home drunk, turn the children out, but they'd say "Aye, he does work." If you worked, it was the crowning glory. You hadn't to be lazy. You had to work all the hours God sent. . . . I suppose it had a good side to it.'

As we talk, I can see why people steeped in this morality of work took against those who, in the 1960s and 1970s, turned up in Hebden with an apparent gospel of taking it easy.

Willie went into a job at Jack Bridge mill. 'I didn't go willingly. But I knew everybody that worked there. It was like a huge family: 240, all local people. All weaving.

'I learnt to weave, then went in the warehouse, then in the office. I was there for thirty years. My mother ran the catering. I never liked weaving. A very laborious and painful job. It went on and on the same. You never got anywhere. Repetition, repetition. My mother's cousin had the mill at that time. Oh, he was naughty, cantankerous – built like a gasometer. He fixed iron plates on the WC seats to deter the weavers from stopping there so long. He used to say "Look after t'weavers. They make tha living, tha knows." But I never heard a word against him, from the weaver's point of view. He went every day to Manchester to get orders. "You can't get orders out of thin air." There was no depression at Jack Bridge.

'Bacon Jim – Jim Uttley – he was a director of Jack Bridge mill. He bought the engine. He was a preacher. He walked everywhere. Everybody knew him. He kept pigs. He sold us bacon when he came to tea. Another mill director was Jim o'Bob's – Jim Stansfield. He'd be selling corn in the mill when trade was bad. Sutcliffe Pickles, from Hebden Bridge: he was another director.

'I was there till the mill closed, then I went to a builder's office. Then I retired. Now I can't do anything. I've even retired from that. This is my grandfather's cane.'

As the sectarian hostility faded, Willie began to preach at all the chapels. 'I went to all of them in turn. I was put on the Plan [the official diary of speakers]. I closed Highgate chapel with the last address. It had got to three old ladies. It had been the seventh largest Baptist church in Great Britain. It held 1,200 people. They performed the *Messiah* every year. I went to speak at all the funerals. Once it was seven in a week. My grandfather's grave is right in front of the Slack chapel door. The sexton said "Suthee [see, you], he's there."

'For a long time I didn't go to the Unitarians. I couldn't understand them. A friend said "Tha'll be all right. On no account mention Christ – he's not part of the Godhead."

'Chapels were in competition. Always wanting to better the others. Even chapels of the same sect – all the Baptists, say – hated one another. Collections were published in the paper. People asked "Are they up or down?" They couldn't go up every year, could they?

'The mill owners had their own chapels. Luddenden Foot chapel was a big monument to the man who ran the mill [the Murgatroyd family]. There was a seat for everyone who worked there. You couldn't work for him unless you went to that chapel. At the end, there were no workpeople. They imported some from Ireland, and the Irish built the Roman Catholic church alongside the Murgatroyd chapel. In Hebden Bridge, Foster Lane was a Redman chapel, Hope Baptists was Crossleys'. Birchcliffe had a hoity-toity crowd.' (One of the Birchcliffe streets was always known as Snob Row.) 'It was the last one built. Enormous. When you addressed the congregation, you couldn't see the people at the back. After I gave my first address there, the superintendent came up to me and said "Thank you, Mr Sutcliffe, very good. But, you know, we don't go a bundle on saints." I'd said the wrong thing. I kept off saints after that.

'The good side of chapels was the social life. But there was lot of back-biting and ill-feeling, a great lack of human kindness. Plain talking can hurt, you know – be very destructive. You think it, but you've no need to say it. As they say, "If you can't say summat good about somebody, say nowt about 'em."'

# 4. STONE

To reach the best place for gathering the sweet green leaves for 'dock pudding', I used to walk along the road to a hamlet which was accurately named Midgehole. When I got there, I went along the side of an old mill and down to a big field on the edge of the river Hebden, just where it emerged from a beautiful wooded valley, Hardcastle Crags.

Up above me, along a lane, was Hawdon Hall, scene of one of the grimmer, but beloved, tales of old Hebden. (The coiners' misdeeds, and eventual retribution, were another oft-told story.) A yew grew next to the old Hawdon Hall farmhouse. Two local men, Old Mike and Joah at Bogg Eggs (a hilltop farm), hid in the tree. Then, after nightfall, they crept out to rob and murder the farmer, Sammy o'Katty's. It was said that every 7 February, the anniversary of the crime, the yew tree oozed with blood. I was told this story regularly, but I never caught the (suitably gloomy) yew as it bled. I always thought that the crime must have taken place some time in, let's say, my grandfather's time. It was years before I found out that the murder happened in 1817.

For my dock gathering I took a large sack, but I could fill it quickly in the riverside field I always went to. Back home, I divided the docks into carrier bags and sold them to neighbours. Many people liked dock pudding, which has a spinachy taste, fried up with their morning bacon – but didn't want the bother of collecting the docks themselves. They were never on sale in shops.

The sweet docks in dock pudding aren't the coarse cow-docks you put on a sting if you hope to soothe it. They're a variety of bistort – of which there's a pretty-looking garden version. Even in the wild, it has small, delicate leaves with a pale pink flower rising up on a stem. It likes to grow somewhere damp.

Dock pudding isn't unique to Hebden, but it's now uncommon anywhere else. *Polygonum bistorta* has a handful of alternative names, including Easter Ledges and Passion Dock – because the dish is eaten around Lent (Passiontide) or Easter, when the leaves are young and tender. In *The Englishman's Flora* (1958), Geoffrey Grigson gives a longish list of these alternatives. But I never heard any of them in Hebden. They were just 'dock pudding docks'. Grigson gives a recipe from the Lake District. But the annual Dock Pudding Festival is now held in Hebden. Each year's winning recipes are duly published in the *Hebden Bridge Times*. They are all much the same. A handful of oatmeal is added to a quart of docks. Onions and a few nettles are the most favoured extra ingredients. Much of the flavour comes from the bacon the dock pudding is fried with. Though it's called a pudding, it's never enclosed in pastry. Like spinach, it is eaten loose on the plate. As a child, I never liked it much, but that didn't deter me from hawking it.

Even if I wanted to, I can't now get to the same gathering ground for docks. The mill has been pulled down and the people who own the nearby farm have put barbed wire along the river line, with 'Private, Keep Out' notices. In my childhood, I never remember either barbed wire or privacy notices anywhere (though I suppose there must have been some). You felt you could wander where you liked.

At Midgehole, there is the entry lodge to the woods. This was built by the Savile family, who at that time owned the entire left bank of the river, as well as the moors up above and a half-hidden side-valley called Crimsworth. Most of the right bank belonged to Abraham Gibson, who lived near Heptonstall. An eighteenth-century mill in the middle of the woods is still called Gibson mill. This is where the Gibson money had come from, but it dwindled away. When 'Ab' died a bachelor, having lived with his mother until her death, his land was bequeathed to the National Trust. Lord Savile had already donated his own stretch of the woodland, though he held on to the shooting lodge and the moors, with their profitable game rights. The first time I ever drank beer was as an adolescent grouse beater. The team of us was picked up in the centre of Hebden Bridge by a Savile truck. Our job was to help drive the birds towards the butts where the shooting party waited. Bottles of beer were handed out at lunch. I didn't like the bitterness.

Ab Gibson was a puzzle to his neighbours. They seldom saw him, except when he walked to Heptonstall church with his mother. Savile, by contrast, was never seen at all. In 1978 I interviewed him at his main house, Gryce Hall, beyond Huddersfield, 20 miles away. He said how fond he was of Hebden, but this wasn't where the main Savile properties were. Most people's main contact with the Savile estate was through his agent and head gamekeeper. A little poaching was commonplace.

To walk through Hardcastle Crags is perhaps my greatest pleasure when I go back to Hebden. The mixed beech and pine woods along the river Hebden were mostly planted by the Saviles, to add to the picturesqueness. There is a special variety of ferocious wood ant, which casts up huge ant hills. The Crags were always seen as a beauty spot. Swiss businesses in Manchester began to hold outings to the place they called 'Little Switzerland'. Before workers got holidays with pay, their only breaks were Sundays and bank holidays. From the nearby towns – Rochdale and Oldham on the Lancashire side, Huddersfield and Bradford on the Yorkshire side – people dressed up and caught the train to Hebden Bridge. From the station you could either walk all the way to the Crags or get on a charabanc – meaning, then, a large horse-drawn cart with wooden benches to sit on. At Gibson mill, long disused, you could picnic or buy a ham tea. For years there was a dance floor on the top storey of the mill. It was then converted to a roller-skating rink. Local men tried to break endurance records. The champion was a skater called Arnold Binns.

For years hardly anyone went up the Crags. But in the mid-1960s, when the Central Electricity Generating Board thought the valley was neglected enough to put huge pylons across the valley, and Halifax corporation thought no one would mind if they covered much of it with a reservoir, these threats gave birth to the Calder Civic Trust. Both projects were halted. Under the National Trust's ownership, visitor numbers have risen. The mill has displays of Industrial Revolution history, chronicling the move from hilltop hand-loom weaving down to water-power mills like this, and then the shift further downstream, nearer to the rail head. There are more car parks than there used to be. But so far the Trust has kept to the ban on cars going any further into the woods. Once you get beyond the mill, you still hardly meet anyone. The peacefulness is soul-soothing.

At the end of the woods, you come out into a narrow junction of two streams, called Blake Dean. I see that a couple have driven here to walk their dog on the waterside patches of grass. The only noise is the soughing of the wind through ash trees and sycamores.

On the slope up towards the moors there are the remains of Blake Dean chapel. The slope was so steep that you came down from an upper road to reach the meeting room, and went up from a lower road to reach the basement room. Hence the little puzzle, always put to children: 'Where is it that you go down to go upstairs and up to go downstairs?' Answer: 'Blake Dean chapel.' Like many chapels, it tottered on with services on special days, especially Easter Sunday. The chapel itself has left hardly a trace. The small old manse is now a scout hut, the door and windows sealed tight with green-painted steel shutters. A few gravestones have survived, even though someone has set up a barbecue in the middle. You read the old names – Shackleton, Rawsthorn, Pickles, Cockcroft, Helliwell, Redman, Farrar, Mitchell, Sheard – nearly all from the 1860s–70s. The grandest memorial is for Harry Lund of New High Laithe farm, Heptonstall, who died at thirty-one. Black marble with the motto, 'In the midst of life we are in death'.

The water of the main stream – the source of the river Hebden – mostly gurgles along through the rocks. Sometimes it goes as slow as treacle. It is deep brown from the iron in the moorland peat. A heron flaps overhead like a stiff mechanical toy. A rabbit's scut vanishes from the side of the path. There are four stone footings from a wooden trestle bridge which once carried a rail line, taking workmen from a temporary settlement of wooden huts near Heptonstall, high across the stream, to build reservoirs among the moors. The disused bridge was pulled down after a young woman fell from it and died.

A pub up the hillside, The Packhorse Inn, is always known as 'The Ridge'. The Pennine Way runs next to it. On one wall of the dining room, a severe-looking photograph shows the man who designed the bridge, William Henry Cockcroft, 1841–1921. He was, among other things, a Methodist lay preacher and a Freemason, it seems. He practised as an architect in Hebden Bridge for fifty years. He was, it's claimed, 'architect of most of the mills, detached houses and chapels of Calderdale.' Probably most of the top-and-bottom terraces, also. In other words, he set the local style. Yet I've never met anyone who's heard of him. He apparently designed the Hebden Bridge chapel I went to, with its 'Russian-inspired onion domes'.

The collection of workmen's huts for the builders of the reservoirs was called Dawson City, after the Klondyke gold rush. It was full of hard-drinking men. It sometimes seems that nothing ever quite vanishes. The Dawson City huts were sold off cheap when the reservoir work finished. Some became shops in Mytholmroyd or Hebden Bridge, by the river edge. One or two of them survived floods and are still there. Another became a house and was gradually modified into a normal-looking bungalow – but you can still see evidence of the original hut if you look closely.

By the Blake Dean stream side, I see two vertical freestanding pillars. One is about five feet high, the other six feet. They are about six paces apart. The pillar on the left has four carefully-cut square sockets. The other pillar has corresponding protrusions. The stones are like surgically separated twins, or would-be lovers. Between the two an ancient beech twists down and overhangs the stream. Another old beech has crashed flat on to the ground. Halfway along the seemingly dead trunk a young beech has grown up out of it. Yggdrasil, the Tree of Life.

In places like this you can see why New Age beliefs might take hold, and there's plenty of that in Hebden now. One bookshop has a rich display of oddball books: *Pagan Resurrection*, for example, *Paranormal West Yorkshire* and *Weird Calderdale*, alongside such worthy magazines as *Herstoria*, *Mslexia* and *The Green Parent*. The best satire of this mumbo-jumbo side of Hebden is John Morrison's locally published *View from the Bridge*. He calls his dopey anti-heroine 'Willow Woman'. All these believers – living on the wilder shores of ecology – are as convinced of rightness as Methodists used to be. In fact, they seem to have the upper hand. Hope Baptist church offers 'Celtic Worship' and a 'Festival of Faith and Spirituality'. But it has very few in its congregation. Upstairs from one of the many bric-a-brac shops in Hebden Bridge, something called 'Mountain of Hope' is advertised. The door is shut when, out of curiosity, I go up. It turns out to offer a 'Tuesday Therapist'. Best not to despair on other days, then.

You can go across Shackleton Hill from Blake Dean, into the Crimsworth Dean side-valley of the river Hebden. Pass the sheep and their grazing lambs, and you reach another stone puzzle: the Cain and Abel stones or, as some call them, Abel Cross. They are two tall single pillars, which lean towards each other. One is marked with a simply carved cross. The nearest farm is called Abel Cote, but there's no telling whether the farm was named after the stones or vice versa. (Another farm, across the Crimsworth valley is called Barker Cote.) The stones are a trigger for New Age musings, or thoughts about unsolved murders. But I've come across a similar pairing in Cheshire, where everyone seems agreed that they are the uprights of church or village crosses pulled down by the iconoclasts of the Reformation and somehow preserved and re-erected by a stubborn believer. In Crimsworth also?

The next farm I come to, Laithe, is still a working farm. Almost all those on this side of the valley have been left by the Savile estate to fall down. Selling or leasing them to outsiders could hinder the profitable grouse shoots. Almost all those on the far side of the valley have been sold, and elaborately renovated. When the great changes in Hebden began, in the late 1960s, you could get seventeenth-century farmhouses for about £600. Nobody wanted them. But at Laithe a young man and his wife are out in the sunshine, playing with their two small children. The wind suddenly turns cold, and they go back inside.

Walking on, I meet head-on a dark-green Land Rover. A man from the estate. We nod and pass by. On the hillside above, Nook farm is collapsing. Further down the lane, Sunny Bank farm has more or less vanished: most of the stone has been sold and removed.

I go on to the cool stream, Crimsworth Dean beck, tippling over rocks in a graceful cascade. This is Lumb Falls. The water creates a pool deep enough to swim in, but only wide enough for a few strokes. Green ferns and dark moss line the cascade. A thin stone bridge crosses the stream at the head of the waterfall. It looks barely strong enough to stay up.

This has always been a place for picnics. A little further upstream is where I first came across Martin Parr, in 1977. I was with my family, enjoying the sun. Our younger children were splashing about in the rocky pools. My father wore a sporty straw hat. A young man came bounding down the stream, clicking his camera. I went down in his wake and caught up with him when he paused. Newly graduated from Manchester art school, Martin and four friends had set up a business in an empty shop in Hebden Bridge, the Albert Street Workshop. In a 'regenerated' Albert Street, the shop now sells fancy ribbons. But the connection is not forgotten. For the 2010 annual arts festival, Martin came to speak to a full audience at the Hebden Bridge Picture House (itself threatened with closure, once, until the council bought it). The arts festival shop displayed some of the affectionate photographs he took while he lived in Hebden. Many were of Crimsworth, its tiny chapel (now a house) and the people who lived round about, on these hills.

Martin Parr's photography was then in the gentle tradition of Henri Cartier-Bresson: still in black and white. He had not yet moved into colour and adopted his later, more ironic style. A couple of days after our chance meeting, I went down to the workshop and picked up a print of our family picture.

Ted Hughes wrote a poem called 'Six Young Men'. It was inspired by a snapshot which had been taken from above the falls. It showed the six young men bathing. The date of the photograph was some time before the First World War broke out. Hughes evokes what may have happened to them later. A little plaque has been set into rock by the Elmet Trust, which commemorates Hughes, at the point where the photograph may have been taken. Lumb Falls is, among other things, a place of memories. I remember sitting beside it with sandwiches in summer heat. That is, heat by Hebden standards. A wooden seat, along from the Elmet plaque, has this inscription: 'Neville. Just another walk with thee/Just another kiss with thee/Just another moment with thee. Helen.'

The former Crimsworth chapel stands a couple of fields above this spot. It was a plain meeting house, attended by plain-speaking people. The congregation must have often sung William Cowper's eighteenth-century hymn, 'Walking with God', which begins:

> O for a closer walk with God,
> A calm and heavenly frame,
> A light to shine upon the road
> That leads me to the Lamb!

This clicks back into my mind as I read the inscription on the seat. It obviously echoes the hymn, which I remember from my own Sunday school days.

I walk back along the old Haworth road, which was by-passed almost two centuries ago by a straighter (but higher) toll road, laid down by a turnpike trust in the newly invented macadamised way. Below the roadside, I pass a series of gentrified farms. Double garages, close-cropped lawns, neatly aligned evergreen shrubs. They guard their privacy. Only one of them bears its name on the roadside gatepost. Gentrification – 'greentrification' – helped to preserve the buildings, but it also drove out working farms. When a farmer dies, his empty house and barn is worth far more to his heirs than his farm business. They sell the property on.

I walk on, past a row of houses called Duck Hill, to the hamlet of Pecket Well, where I've borrowed a terraced cottage. No one quite knows why the place got its name. The most plausible is that it is named after Thomas à Becket, the patron saint of Heptonstall church, which you can see right across the valley. (This is the tall Victorian church. Its medieval predecessor is a romantic ruin in the church grounds.) But this may be folk-etymology.

Pecket is now stripped-out from most of its old functions. Two farms are for sale, Clough Head and Wilcroft. The primary school has been pulled down, and only the old school house is still standing. Two large bungalows, Nook and Carnaby, have been built on the rest of the site. There was a Co-op, and the plate-glass frontage is still there. It became a sort of community college for a while, but it now has a 'for sale' sign. The two biggest structures were the huge, grim chapel, with its freestanding Sunday school – now a house and flats – and Pecket Shed, the last of the Hebden fustian mills to stay in use – but now also converted into flats. A carved date above the entrance arch announces that it was built in 1858. It closed in 1998. Strangely, some of the mills stayed on the hilltops when others had shifted towards the rail head.

Pecket still has its pub, the Robin Hood. The toll bar keeper's cottage is also still here. Birdsong fills the air. The fields are full of buttercups (it has apparently been a good year for them). You can see Hardcastle Crags woods below, like a green wave. I take a bridle path down towards an obelisk-shaped war memorial which overlooks Midgehole.

The track, between dry-stone walls, is little used. It is thick with cow dock, nettles and butterflies. The obelisk, the tower of Heptonstall church and, on a far hill, another, much bigger obelisk are lined up like sitting ducks. The second, older obelisk is Stoodley Pike, originally built to commemorate the end of the Napoleonic Wars, which allowed British textiles to be exported into continental Europe again.

The track emerges at a cluster of houses: Crimsworth Farm, Lower Crimsworth, Crimsworth Cottages. '1661' is carved, with an awkward hand, over one door. I'd walked down, partly, because I'd seen, from the upper road, some small, lively black animals scurrying around. The woman who's been feeding them comes out through the field gate. She tells me they are black Berkshire piglets. Every year she feeds two batches of the pigs till they are big enough to be sold on. She also has some black Maran hens: 'good layers'. She is cheerful, crop-haired, unaggressive towards my barging-in. She tells me she is off this day through illness. When she isn't a part-time pig and hen breeder, she is a full-time IT manager at the University of Leeds library. Unasked, she mentions her partner: 'She works in a café down Hebden Bridge.' I can hardly ask for a neater model of the new Hebden.

A young man, Ben Plumpton, is working on a new plantation of trees alongside the track, on the edge of the National Trust's Hardcastle Crags land. A label tells me it's called, rather grandiosely, White Rose Forest. One of Hebden's many charities is called Treesponsibility. It presses on with the job of recladding the Calder valley with trees, which was pioneered by the Civic Trust. But this is private-enterprise planting.

Besides eco-folk, Hebden is well populated with peaceniks of one kind or another. (Often the same people.) The visitor information centre, down on the Rochdale canal wharf beside the Picture House, sells one postcard which shows the CND symbol painted white on a local field. But nothing comes easy, not even peace. The obelisk I'm now standing by is often known as Little Stoodley Pike. It was put up by the parish council to honour 'those who offered all for the sacred cause of world peace'. From the First World War, thirty-four deaths are recorded; six for the Second World War. All the usual surnames, from Ashworth to Wild, by way of Crabtree, Greenwood, Redman and Sutcliffe. Wherever I find them, I increasingly see these names as a litany of Hebden-ness.

# 5 . FAMILY

Chris Ratcliffe is one of the original Hebden 'hippies' (to use the local label from those days). He's been here since May 1975. In the late 1970s he took part in a much-contested squat in a row of perfectly habitable houses which were scheduled for demolition. The squatters won. The Queen's Terrace houses are still there, on the road up to Heptonstall. The squatters' victory drew the final line under further house demolition schemes. Chris is now in his mid-sixties. He agrees that it's a bit difficult to claim to be a hippie at this age. But he still has something of that attractive aura.

I've come to meet him, in the summer of 2010, at the house he shared with his partner, Elaine Connell, until she died of cancer two and a half years back. As we speak, he is waiting for a phone call from his son, who is at Cambridge, to let him know what grade of degree he got. It's a 2:1 – which, it seems, is fine. The son moved from Calder High School to a Huddersfield 'sixth-form college' before he won a Cambridge place. It sounds a bit like a crammer's. Chris explains that this was Elaine's wish, in order to give their son every chance. I listen sympathetically. I have heard such stories many, many times. Chris and Elaine, along with some other local hippies in Hebden and elsewhere, gave their son the surname 'Wild' – that is, roving free – to help cast off the shackles of family. But family nearly always wins. Chris says there was a TV documentary about the naming business, called *The Wild Things*. He also tells me that his newly graduated son calls him 'a professional hippie'.

I like Chris a lot, though I wouldn't want to be at the wrong end of a campaign he led. He lives on a row of top-and-bottom houses: Windsor Road on the top side, Windsor View underneath. Windsor View is where my mother's family moved, to save money on rent, when my grandfather died of flu. The 2002 academic research into Hebden greentrification includes some revealing interviews with estate agents – which are among the most prominent local shops now, and whose ads keep the *Hebden Bridge Times* in business. One of the agents said: 'Oh, if we get any arty or hippie types looking for a place to live, we always send them along to the Windsors. It's best if they all stay together.'

Windsor Road has all the signs of this quietly pursued apartheid policy. Windows overflow with house plants. Inside, you see glimpses of vivid posters. A large van belonging to a band called Rhythm Bridge is parked on the roadside (rather to Chris's annoyance); the drummer lives here. Chris has lived on Windsor Road since 1989. There are stretches of grass at each side. He led a campaign to see off developers here – and safeguard the Windsor residents' outlook – by setting up a charity to buy the land and protect it. We sit and have fresh-brewed coffee together on the stone-flagged pavement outside his house, enjoying the sun. His hair and beard are grey now. He wears jeans, canvas shoes and a black sweater. 'Just look around,' he says. 'Hebden is a perfect combination of urban and rural.'

His father was a cinema manager. Chris left school to work as a clerk, and met students who inspired him to take A-levels. He was at the University of Essex, when this campus led what passed for student revolution in Britain in the late 1960s. He went over to France for the May 1968 'events', which genuinely did rock a regime. He moved into squats in Hackney, edited the *Hackney Gutter Press* and worked with the local claimants' union. In the late 1970s he trained as a teacher and taught 'social studies' at a further education college in Halifax and in a secondary modern school ('an uphill battle'). He remained 'a Luddite' in the 1970s, he says, and 'occupied computer rooms.' The theory was that computers destroyed work in the same way that machines destroyed hand-loom weaving.

The irony is that his recent life has been strongly dedicated to the computer. With Elaine he set up an online publishing house, Pennine Pens; in 1995 he created a community website; he now makes his living mostly as a website designer and from selling books. The most entertaining book he publishes is John Morrison's *View from the Bridge*. This began as an online column on the community website, mocking the idiosyncrasies and pretensions of the now-ageing ex-hippies. Morrison used to live in Hebden

Bridge but has now moved on. He obviously knew, all too well, what he was talking about.

The website's forum was launched as a sort of offcomer counterblast to the then strongly localist *Hebden Bridge Times*. Chris protested to the paper's owners that it ignored arts events and environmental issues. The paper certainly doesn't do that now. But Chris acknowledges the local/offcomer divide, and how the politics of it has worked. 'We run the place now.' It is symptomatic that, as we speak, only two members of the town council are local. Nicola Jones, who chairs a revivified Calder Civic Trust, says that 'about 50 people are on all the local committees' and few of these (including Nicola herself) are local in the fullest sense. 'Two things have helped to bring prosperity: the arts and new technology,' Chris says. 'People working from home, adding up to hundreds of small businesses – that's probably the biggest industry around here.'

Hebden is now a major supplier of letters to the *Guardian*. All those people sitting, lonely, at their computers? The forum has a similar angry-liberal tone. As with any local paper, planning and development are the issues that get the contributors hottest under the collar. A certain offcomer nimbyism has crept in: 'what we have we hold'. And undeniably the pressures to build are very great. Walking around the hills, it is extraordinary how many houses have been tucked into bits and pieces of land. 'Before the crash of 2008, every little bit of space was subject to development,' Chris says. These new houses are where the second wave of arrivals live: those for whom Hebden Bridge is mainly a nice place to commute from. The first wave react to them in much the same way as the locals reacted to the their own arrival. With deep suspicion. What goes around comes around.

I walk across Hebden Bridge to see Mike Barrett, who's a good friend of Chris Ratcliffe's. Mike is a graphic designer; his firm is called frogsdesign. I had seen his name on a delightful set of postcards of Hebden Bridge, published in 2010 to mark '500 Years of Creativity' in Hebden. The idea for such a celebration was Mike's. He got it from a date, 1510, carved into an arch of the old bridge. There was probably a wooden bridge here earlier. Even for the stone bridge '1510' may have marked a repair job. It is also true that, at that date, there were very few buildings down in the valley – perhaps an inn or two and a corn mill. Not yet much by way of creativity.

Most of the population lived up on the hills, and creativity meant weaving by hand.

But it was a brilliantly inventive piece of publicity, linking the off-comers back into local history. No one else, ever, so far as I know, had ever thought of Hebden Bridge in that way. It was the invention of a tradition. Mike created posters in which the typography cleverly echoed the spiky, amateurish lettering on the 1510 carving. As you drove into Hebden, Mike's attractive poster-work announced the quincentenary. Only as you left did you see that the reverse side of the post said, 'That was *so* Hebden Bridge.' If the first wave of offcomers needed a motto, this was it.

Mike is one of the home workers Chris has been talking about. He lives in a house in that part of Hebden Bridge, Birchcliffe, which is nearly all top-and-bottom houses. This almost always forms the backdrop to the usual photographs. He welcomes me in. Sandals, bald head, first-rate coffee. We sit in the kitchen to talk. Socks and underpants are drying on a creel pulled up to the ceiling.

In the 1960s he studied for a science degree at what is now the University of Bradford. He went on to teach sciences at a school and in art college. In Bradford he lived in a commune and helped to produce a community newspaper. He turned his hand to all kinds of things. He was a mental health nurse. He drew cartoons. He bought old furniture and painted it up for resale. But it was hard to make a steady living that way. 'For graphics, people would pay by the hour.' Like Chris, Mike is in his sixties. Two of his children are now over 40; two are teenagers. His present partner is away as we talk; so is one of the children. The other is upstairs, revising for A-levels. Mike moved to Hebden in 2002, because 'I hoped it would become a kind of ethos. A small community, self-sufficient, with an artistic input. People are doing incredible things in their back room. A lot of nice people live in Hebden Bridge.' He acknowledges that many of them are 'branded as offcomers, by the Greenwoods and so on. I would like to see more integration. But life is pretty good, really.'

Before we part he takes me up to the edge of a chapel graveyard where he and his partner have set up an allotment society. For £100, they bought the graveyard itself, taking on an obligation to tend it, and laid out the allotments. They now have a patch each and the others are rented out. I admire the onions, which are coming along nicely.

# 6. HIPPO

'If a thing isn't in Hebden Bridge, it isn't worth bothering with.' Christine Jackson is our neighbour in Pecket Well, charming and shrewd. As a student, I delivered Christmas post with her father, Harold – originally from Salford – who drove one of the parcel delivery vans. She now works as secretary to the town mayors – as the leaders of parish councils can now choose to be renamed. She takes a calm but very Hebden view of the various people who turn up with their own agendas. 'A lot come in, saying "I'm Hebden Bridge," and I just . . .' She breaks off to act out a yawn. 'They come and go. Hebden Bridge goes on.'

She is devoted to Hebden Bridge, where she grew up on a hillside council estate, and to her job. She and her husband Ronnie are about to set off on an annual parish boundary walk.

'You get people who've lived in the area a long time,' she says, 'and they cherish the freedom to be yourself and still be accepted. Hebden keeps attracting people. What rubs is when they want to change things – and then go. But Hebden *is* a community, it's a pioneering place, starting doing new things. People catch up with us later. There are different strands. Some leave Hebden Bridge because it isn't how it was. But I have this weird sense of love of Hebden. You have to embrace this new Hebden Bridge.'

The Jacksons' two sons live only a few miles away. But not in Hebden Bridge, where house prices rise and rise. And for all the picturesqueness of the top-and-bottom houses, she notes, 'A lot of people move down to Mytholmroyd [which today is Hebden Bridge's own suburb] when they're older. Into houses that are more modern, more convenient.'

Sometimes, downtown Hebden Bridge seems like an extension of Covent Garden by other means. Nigel Waterhouse is sitting at the end of the packhorse bridge, in a gentle drizzle, playing his accordion. When he was only seven, he wanted an accordion for Christmas. His musical career took him into various orchestras, he says, including Opera North's in Leeds. He travels around, to Halifax or to Keighley. He shakes his curls in the damp, but strikes up a sprightly folkish tune. 'Busking can be quite nice,' he says, 'but there are now too many buskers around.' He has lived in Hebden for fourteen years. He is in his fifties. His partner is a piano tuner.

Just across the street, Tim Gibbons is clowning around in a leaf-green suit and a tall yellow hat. His act is more Marcel Marceau than Barnum & Bailey. Very fey. He bends to peer into a street grating, then walks across to talk. In Maidstone, Kent, he tells me, he worked with a doctor who used clowning as part of his mental health work. Before that, Tim was a drama teacher. Now he often works at 'facilitating different groups, helping with stigma, confronting the issues about multiple sclerosis, acting out scenarios'. He describes this as 'enabling theatre' or 'the theatre of the oppressed'. He has lived in Hebden for fifteen years. He is a few months younger than Nigel Waterhouse.

When Hebden Bridge celebrated its 500 years of creativity in summer 2010, one of the most photogenic sights was a huge grey hippopotamus and a chirpy green dragon, making their way across the packhorse bridge. They led a procession of people, pushing, carrying or wearing the fantastic parade-art they'd made at a special open-to-all workshop. The idea of an annual 'Hebden Bridge Handmade Parade' was the brainwave of a wondrous organisation called Thingumajig Theatre. The first parade was held in 2008.

Thingumajig was founded by a Korean-American puppeteer, Andrew Kim, and a British actress and musician, Kathy Bradley, who first worked together in 2002 as mask performers. To begin with, their theatre work often took them far apart. Then they decided to make their relationship less long-distance and live on the same continent as each other. They married, and set up shop as Thingumajig in an old chapel near Pecket, called Wainsgate. Andrew does much of the puppet building. Kathy writes scripts, plays music (she studied flute at the Royal Academy of Music) and sews costumes.

I begin talking to them in a big shed lent to them for the parade. Andrew wears tan chinos and a black T-shirt. Kathy wears a boiler suit. Their faces light up as they talk about the puppets.

The dragon, whose name is Veronica, leans sloppily against one wall. It takes two people inside to work her. 'She's good bread and butter for us,' Andrew says. 'Very bouncy and lively. Light silk, hand-dyed. She's quite a celebrity in Hebden Bridge.' 'She's beautiful and poetic as well,' Kathy says. 'Very effervescent. She likes to dance.' It's 'all like asking people to enter your world of make-believe,' Kathy says. A woman came up to them one day and asked if Veronica was real. 'She's a special local citizen. They know her by name.'

The hippo, whose name is Hieronymus, stands tall in the middle of the shed. He hasn't yet been dismantled. He is built on to a wheeled base, like a bicycle. It's true that the puppets develop personalities as you look at them. Kathy talks about them almost as if they are children. Andrew is in his forties, she is ten years older. 'The hippo has only performed twice in Hebden Bridge so far,' she says. 'He's feeling a bit poorly. But they come alive as we perform. They each have their own character. Who knows what's next?'

Andrew is Korean by birth, but his parents moved to the United States when he was six. He learnt the puppetry business in America – in Minneapolis and Seattle especially, where puppet parades were well-established. He is the artistic director of the annual Handmade Parades. Collaborative by nature, he emphasises that other top-rank puppet-makers also take part. Each year the Hebden Bridge parade is divided into three or four sections, each under a 'lead artist'. Thingumajig runs one section direct.

This shed where I'm visiting Andrew and Kathy was Thingumajig's public workshop. Anyone could come and create their own parade wear, either from material they brought themselves, or from some held here. 'The parade is the jewel in our work,' Andrew says. 'People can come and make whatever they want.'

Andrew and Kathy are very much a couple, picking up on each other's words and thoughts. I see them next in their Wainsgate chapel base, getting ready for a more traditional puppet show in York.

The chapel is down a rough track, behind trees. Growing up in Hebden, I never knew where it was. The graveyard has two tall marble columns, one for Ashworths, one for Redmans, side by side, with draped urns above. One corner seems to specialise in babies and young children, the most recent were buried here in 1999. Also: Alex Kwasi Sarkodee-Adoo was buried here in 1991. A extraordinary and unexpected name. Who was he?

The chapel is a huge square shed on the outside. Inside this ashlar box, it is like a delicate jewel. It is a real temple, now preserved by the Historic Chapels Trust and listed Grade II-starred. The memorial windows commemorate various Mitchells. A few hundred yards away, the Mitchell family cotton mill is one of the few tall black chimneys left standing, a landmark for many miles. One of the more recent tenants – originally a hippyish enterprise – makes circus equipment. The mill is dated 1851. The chapel is 1856. The local cricket club (1894), next to the mill, is still flourishing, though it got into trouble with the local cricket board when three of its players suddenly left to celebrate Eid and the team had to perform short-handed for a big match. The local Co-op (1906), built in an odd triangular shape, to fit a field corner, and now a house, completes the picture of a vanished world.

One further social footnote. Just down the hill from the old Co-op is a nineteenth-century terraced row called Club Houses. Such houses were built for, and often by, workers who put their joint savings together in order to erect them. (Others, locally, seized on a wider ambition and formed an America Club.) These projects were the first glimmer of the building society business. The terrace houses are now all gentrified. Across the road from this attractive relic of self-help is a 1940s council house estate, put together out of prefabricated concrete slabs. These houses are not gentrified.

At Wainsgate, Andrew and Kathy have their base in the downstairs of the old Sunday school, behind the chapel. Upstairs, an art show by local painters is being dismantled. (The chapel itself is used for concerts.) The Thingumajig workshop is a treasure trove. The parade puppets like Veronica the dragon and Hieronymus the hippo have all been folded up and tucked into their nests along the back wall. Other puppets lie half-done, awaiting their next touch of paint or new bit of sewing. Andrew and Kathy are brushing up their memories of the script of their travelling show, *A November Day*, and making sure all the puppets are in good working order.

*A November Day* is a fable about the First World War. Thingumajig created it in 2008, to mark the 90th anniversary of the war's end. But people continue to want to see it. It is about one survivor's memories of the conflict – partly based on Kathy's grandfather's own memories – and his encounter with a stray dog which knew no boundaries between the Allied and German lines. Andrew picks up a soldier puppet, with large papier-mâché hands, closed eyes and a heavy grey coat. Right away, the puppet seems, movingly, to come to life. The Thingumajig rehearsal is about to start. I tiptoe out.

Andrew, Kathy and the man I visit next, Andy Plant, stay out of Hebden politics altogether. They want to get on with their work. Behind the façade of 'community', there are rival squadrons of groups and counter-groups. One man puts it like this: 'At first this was a broadminded place. Everyone was broadminded. Now the broad-mindedness takes a different form: a different organisation for every strand.' Or as one young woman puts it: 'Hebden isn't always as nice a place as it looks.'

Andy Plant gives me careful instructions on how to reach him. I need them. I drive up a steep winding road. It's like something out of an illustration to a fairy tale. I go past Winters Farm to Winters Cottages. Today the sun shines, but I can see that at other times the names must seem very apt.

Andy is a glorious inventor of magical creations. I first came across his name in an opera programme in London. The English National Opera decided to have a production of Donizetti's *L'Elisir d'Amore* – the elixir of love. The director was Jude Kelly, who then ran the West Yorkshire Playhouse in Leeds. She wanted to have the opera's quack doctor, Dulcemara, arrive on stage in a clapped-out car. He would get out, and the car would fall apart, explosively. She asked Andy to design it. He did, and it was a wonderful moment for the audience.

Andy was born in Sheffield. He went to art school in Birmingham. He then ran a gift business, selling wooden toys through ads at the back of *Private Eye*. He came to Hebden in 1983, making props for a far-left touring theatre group, Welfare State. Hence the Jude Kelly connection. But the big turning point was when he was commissioned to build a water clock for Covent Garden. He loves clocks, the bigger the better.

'A clock is one way of framing a story. There's a performance every hour or quarter-hour. People will gather for it.' It is an idea with more tradition behind it in continental Europe than in Britain.

He likes doing up old buildings. He first lived a bit lower down the hillside in an old mill in a side-valley, Jumble Hole Clough. The planners okayed it as a half-living, half-working space. The alternative, after all, was that the mill would fall down. He moved to these cottages four years ago. He's in his mid-fifties with a four-year-old son. He needed more space, he said. The move also puts him nearer to one of the best-thought-of local primary schools.

He shows me a video of his projects. Many are designed to give some life to vast regeneration schemes. A reflective pool outside a hospital, with waves and leaping fish. A magic garden with mechanised dogs and trees. A comical triumphal arch. A pyrotechnic wheel, 50 feet across, for a Stockton-on-Tees festival: 'People loved it, and just cheered.'

It occurs to me that many of the designs are like animated cartoons. I suggest Gary Larson's strip, *The Far Side*. Andy nods with pleasure. He says he's much influenced by 1930s–50s cartoons. He loves *The Far Side* but hasn't yet used it as a direct source.

He shows me his garden, which is built within the walls of an old dam. Protected, the flowers flourish, even at Winters Cottages. We walk through to his workshop. It could be an engineering shed. Andy collects old lathes. The smell of the lubricating oil reminds me of a small munitions works in Mytholmroyd, which my father was drafted to, during the Second World War, to make bullets. (His pseudonym, for the benefit of the bookie's runner who picked up bets before betting shops were legalised, was 'Bullets & Chips'.) Andy and I discover a mutual regret that in Britain – as opposed to, say, America or France – engineering is so little written up or praised.

Before we part, we share our delight in a current television series which has portrayed in close, fascinating detail the building of a nuclear submarine and of a Rolls-Royce jet engine. I then plunge off down the lane back into the valley.

# 7. ZION

The Primitive Methodist chapel, Mount Zion, looked out over the Rochdale canal at Mytholmroyd. In the 1930s, the various rival strands of Methodism merged. The tiny doctrinal differences hardly seemed worth it when the pressure of secularism was driving congregations down. But for many years the buildings remained. Mytholmroyd had two chapels still, the Wesleyans and the Primitives. The Wesleyans regarded themselves as a step up. The Primitives were more democratic. Their congregation ruled, and elected its ministers directly. When the sect was founded, its hellfire message appealed especially to mining villages and industrial towns, which other preachers had neglected.

In Hebden, when I lived there, there were places of worship for Anglicans, Roman Catholics, Spiritualists, Christadelphians and Jehovah's Witnesses, but the core creeds were Nonconformist: varieties of Baptist and Methodist. 'In most places, when people are asked to put down what religion they have, if any, they say "C. of E.",' an Anglican vicar of Heptonstall once told me. 'Here they say, "Methodist". I've never come across anywhere like this.' Socially, the Baptists regarded themselves as top dogs, but I don't think anyone else agreed with that.

This Nonconformist cast of mind continues. One of the most active ministers in today's valley is Canon James Allison, the vicar of Mytholmroyd. He is an elected member of the town council which, under the name 'Hebden Royd', covers both Hebden Bridge and Mytholmroyd. Until recently, he was a governor of Calder High School (into which my grammar school was merged in 1950, as one of the very first comprehensives). He chairs or takes part in all kinds of local organisations, including the Elmet Trust.

James Allison is very amicable, rather dishevelled-looking. His view of an established church is all-embracing. 'It should be open to everybody. For example, I baptise any children, without questioning whether the parents are married or are Anglican.' But when he has tried to change other things within the church, 'you may hear "Oh, we can't do Lent, it's what the Catholics do, we do Easter," or "We don't do children's worship, the Methodists do that."'

When I turn up to see him, he is holding a small early-morning prayer meeting, in a side room, with three church helpers. The setting looks rather like a health centre. It is called, oddly, the Church Enterprise Centre, and the hall can be hired out. Notices advertise bell-ringing and 'Celebrating Palestinian Culture in Calderdale'. The new centre is on the site of the old Church Institute ('the 'Tute'). On the upper floor, you could play dominoes, cribbage or snooker: but no gambling and no drinking. At the 'Tute, I sometimes helped to set up the triangle of reds for the start of a snooker game of my father's. I also hid a map of hidden treasure in a cleft in the old wall, for later generations to find. (Cautiously, I didn't hide any treasure.) This bit of wall has been demolished. A new car park has been laid out, with a supposedly symbolic sculpture. The script on the base says 'Moors are a stage for the performance of Heaven.' As I note this down, a man comes up to me with his bag of shopping. 'Are you giving it marks out of ten? Seems a bit of a waste of money, to me.' And he walks off.

James claims a congregation of about eighty on a Sunday. 'It's so hard to win people because of the kind of Methodism that prevailed round here. It was based on fear of the Lord, not on God's grace. He agrees with Lady Willie that it was a gospel of work. Outside, in the church graveyard, he shows me one grave which says that the dead man left the earth 'after a strenuous life'. For another, 'now the labourer's task is over'.

A few days earlier, I'd gone to Mytholmroyd church because, as part of the annual Hebden Bridge arts festival, it was showing F.W. Murnau's classic silent Dracula film, *Nosferatu*. And showing it in the nave. I was astonished by this. But James thinks it is 'all part of giving the nave back to the community'.

I go along, partly because I've never seen the film, but also to see who the audience are. The church is a very plain Victorian Gothic, with pitchpine pews and a brass eagle on the lectern. The audience is like a campus film society, twenty years on. These are the new Briggers and Royders. I can only hear the slightest of Yorkshire accents. I have quite a palaver to get in, because I've not pre-booked. It is all right in the end. I sit at the aisle end of a fairly empty row. A party of severe-faced women come in, late, to fill up the rest of the row, each with a glass of red wine in hand. The evening opens with the sort of organ music you might expect to hear at a funeral.

The best thing about the film is that it has a genuinely terrifying Dracula. The worst thing is that, towards the end, the projector breaks down a couple of times. Some of the script seems doubly strange inside a church. For example, 'You've hurt yourself – the precious blood!' But there is nothing Christian, or even very charitable, at this event. At the back of the nave, to try to sign up donors as we leave, are representatives of the National Blood Service. I see no one pause to commit themselves as we go past. Me neither, I confess.

The upper Calder valley has seen much change in its population over the past forty years. But one thing has not changed. Unlike many former textile districts, it is very white-skinned. The Hebden mills were, of course, already running down during the heyday of black and brown immigration. Most such newcomers went elsewhere, where the work was. But even in Hebden it was hard to get local workers to do the remaining night shifts. At first, east Europeans, displaced by the war, did these jobs: Poles, Ukrainians, Lithuanians. After them came the Kashmiris. But these Asian workers went to the back streets of Halifax to sleep. James Allison's wife works as a teacher at a largely Asian school in Halifax. She encouraged the idea of a school trip to Hebden Bridge. 'But, miss, we'd be stared at.' The school trip took place, 'and they were stared at.'

The Calder High School 2011 A-level results include eighteen students with Asian names: about one in six. All these students, I assume, are coming in by bus from Halifax. 'Hebden Bridge is the most racist place I've ever been in,' I am told by one offcomer. This is a wild exaggeration. But one of the unspoken factors causing Hebden to gain popularity, I'd acknowledge, is white flight from cities like Bradford, Leeds and Manchester.

The day after the film and my conversation with James Allison, I go for a walk in the pale sunshine – from Mytholmroyd up to Bell Hole.

This is a steep hollow in the hills. The landscape is wonderfully deserted. I pass Hoo Hole, a working farm with a Tolkienesque name, and on through river-edge fields called Parrock – which sound more C.S. Lewis than Tolkien. The few farms along the way up into the hills used to be inhabited by farmers who specialised in major rows about sheep-runs. Sometimes to the extent of murder. Now, as in Crimsworth, these farms are visibly gentrified. The gardens are well-kempt, the doors of the converted barns are full-glazed. The tidiness is almost unnatural. Along the path through the woods I tread on the stones which were laid for pack-horses and for workers coming down to work. This is Cragg Vale. The mills, once so notorious, have long gone.

The woods begin with fine beeches, then oaks and birch. Little streams run across the path. They are good for children to dam up. Much of the path side is lined with bilberry bushes. I feel immersed in greenness.

Bell House, on the very edge of the moor, was the coiners' head-quarters. David Hartley lived here. I always knew the house was there but, though I had visited Bell Hole many times, I first got as far up as Bell House in the 1970s when an eccentric poet, Gordon Hoyles, was living in it. He was one of the first wave of offcomers. They called themselves 'alternatives' then.

He looked like a cross between Walt Whitman and a tramp. He was heavy-bodied, with wild hair and a long beard. Bell House, like many of the cottages down in the valley, was derelict when he moved in, with the help of a bank loan. No one had lived there for forty years. He had stayed on, so far, for five. His wife had left him. He was now living with 'Blossom' – a small, sparkly blonde – who brought some money in as a cleaner at Calder High School. They were broke, he told me, until she got her first wage packet, next day.

Gordon told me he grew up in Garstang, on the edge of the Yorkshire Dales, and trained as an engineer, then went away to sea. He was thinking of selling Bell House, if he could get the right price. 'I'm getting too old for this sort of life. I'm forty-one.' He had moved around a lot. In London, he lived in shared flats, communes or squats. 'There was always some money somewhere in London. I've never been broke in the way I am now.' He was delighted that an 'alternative' print shop planned to publish his collection of poems, *The Tin Book*. He had written out some of the poems on sheets of tin from an old cooker and old central heating gear. One of them was called 'Hebden Bridge':

> Nestling in a difficulty
>     rent in England's earth
> Need provoked a settlement
>     endurance proved its worth
>
> Angular steep and craggy
>     dwellings stand the tilt
> Linked by tangled track
>     stack on stack and solid built
>
> Step by step strugglings record
>     sculpted living grit
> As grim determination makes
>     The best a better bit.

He was very pleased with the punch lines in some of his poems:

> Conserve energy, do less
> (which is a dig at his fellow-alternatives)
> Destroy the working class
> (which means that he thinks the old style of work is wrong).

Even the singing of the birds, which he asked me to stop and listen to, didn't relieve the barrenness. The barn on one side of Bell House had recently collapsed. A moorland stream was running through it. We went into the house through a door that was off its hinges. The floor was stone-flagged. He and Blossom had built a stone pillar to hold up the main roof beam. A newspaper cutting about Hoyles as 'the hermit poet' was pinned on the wall. Gordon himself was a great writer of scathing letters to the *Hebden Bridge Times*.

Outside, a little maze had been cut into the turf. There was a kind of hippie festival here, a couple of summers before. 'They said I should fence the edge of Bell Hole off. Otherwise, they'd all go flying off. But I'm very much against drugs.' In a rough-and-ready cold frame he could grow broccoli and courgettes, he said. In one of his fields, sods had been turned, to try to create more top soil. But the earth was very thin here. Reeds and bracken were invading. 'I began to wonder if bracken was a tree, there's so much of it; and what we see is just the leaves.

'There are a lot of constraints, living in a community like this,' he said. 'When I was drinking a lot at the pub down in Cragg, I'd use some obscenities and it was all over Mytholmroyd next morning. But I think that those constraints are part of the point, part of the advantage, of living here.'

When *The Tin Book* was published, he sent me a copy. For many years it was lost, but I've now found it again.

# 8. LOCALS

The Morgan family, who ran the Primitive Methodist chapel until the building was sold off for its stone, had obviously come from Wales at some point. Billy Hughes's family must have had a similar origin, before he settled down, for a while near, the chapel. His old house – his son Ted's birthplace – now belongs to the Elmet Trust and you can rent it as a holiday home. Ted Hughes went from here to Burnley Road school before his father moved on to the mining town of Mexborough, near Doncaster, to open a newsagent's. Billy eventually came back. I remember him as a Hebden Bridge tobacconist, in a small shop next to a smithy.

What does 'local' mean? In Hebden, there were several Joneses, also presumably Welsh in origin. They included the newsagent for whom I used to deliver morning papers: mostly the *Yorkshire Post* and *Daily Telegraph* (Tory), *News Chronicle* (Liberal) and *Daily Mirror* (Labour). One of the Mytholmroyd village carriers, with his horse and cart, was called Trewartha, a Cornish name. He played bowls with my father. It was my midday Sunday job in Mytholmroyd to go along to the bowls club, a couple of hundred yards away on the other side of a railway line, and say that lunch was ready. But it was more interesting to me that one field along the way was a good place for digging out the peanut-like edible tubers of 'pignut'. It took some practice to tell this rarer, lacy-flowered umbellifer, *Conopodium majus*, from the omnipresent cow parsley, whose roots bear no such delicacies.

When we moved to Hebden Bridge after the Second World War, our next-door neighbours were a family that had moved down from County

Durham, and kept a slight trace of a Geordie accent. This was unusual enough, but Scots were even rarer. The only Scot I can recall was a red-faced ex-Royal Medical Corps doctor, who was our GP. Looking back on this, I think that Scots who were looking for work between the wars jumped over Yorkshire and Lancashire and went further south – to the new car factories of Ford (Dagenham), Vauxhall (Luton), Austin (Birmingham) and Morris (Oxford). In Luton in the 1930s, a survey of the local social dilemmas focused on the huge intake of Scots at the car works. The author wondered if, with their strange accents, the Scots would ever integrate.

In Hebden, the newcomers at that time came in ones and twos. They usually came from a similar working class, chapel-going background. There were some more exotic arrivals, like the Eurasian family called Ashman who lived on a large Mytholmroyd council estate, or the Poles who after fighting in the British army in the war settled down with upper Calder valley brides. These were absorbed, unquestioned. Unlike the 'invaders' of the late 1960s and 1970s, none was ever seen as an alien force.

The Irish were a partial exception. This was because many had arrived, way back, as labourers, building the canal and the railway, or else as lower-paid workers in the cotton mills; had larger families; and were mostly Roman Catholic. They were still seen as somehow separate. Before farm work was fully mechanised, some still came over from Ireland every summer to help get the harvest in. They went each payday to the post office to buy money orders and mail much of their earnings back home. They were seen as exotic.

In his 1964 novel, *The Jealous God* – now all but forgotten – John Braine chronicled the recurrent strain of anti-Catholicism in the West Riding. It undoubtedly existed. In such cities as Glasgow and Liverpool, this religious divide led to sharp social and political enmity. In Yorkshire, it was all lower-key, but the Catholic form of worship and the power of the priest were a long way from what went on in Methodist chapels. Mass was still celebrated in Latin. Armed with the threat of excommunication, the priests did everything they could to make it difficult for a Roman Catholic to marry a Protestant. If they did marry, a promise to bring the children up as Catholics was demanded. The

1. *My parents' wedding (1931) at a hilltop Baptist chapel near Heptonstall. Left to right: my mother's brother, Tom; my mother (née Marion Ashworth) and my father, Donald Barker; my father's sister, Marjorie (later my favourite aunt) and my father's brother, George. Years afterwards, my sister Elaine was married at the same chapel, now closed. In the new Hebden Bridge, it narrowly escaped becoming the headquarters of a white witch.*

*2. Watching mills burn down was a regular form of local entertainment. (I loved it.)*
*The wooden floors were impregnated with oil from looms. This was one of the last to go:*
*Murgatroyds' Mill, which once employed 2,000 people.*

*3. My parents knew this early cinema as 'the fleapit'. It was one important destination for*
*young men and women, when they weren't on the 'monkey run' evening parade between*
*Hebden Bridge and neighbouring Mytholmroyd.*

*4. Happy days. Children photographed in Church Street, Heptonstall, in 1921. In the mid-twentieth century, the population of this hilltop village gradually aged. Houses fell vacant. From the 1970s, newcomers settled in. Heptonstall school is full of children again, but with few of the traditional local surnames. The children on the seesaw are, from left to right: Sarah Alice Wadsworth, Margaret Gill, Mary Greenwood, Richard Greenwood, Geoff Sunderland, Alice Marsland, Sarah Greenwood, Winnie Holt and Ida Sunderland. (The dog is Mick.)*

5. *Women sew corduroy and fustian (on piece rates) at Nutclough mill, Hebden Bridge. The overseers were men, but the women had economic power. This textile firm began as one of Britain's few successful worker cooperatives. A portrait of the founder-manager, Joseph Greenwood, hangs in the town hall. The mill now houses an electronics company.*

6. *In 1907, during a long strike by textile workers, the suffragette leader Emmeline Pankurst came to town. The strikers' brass band led a procession. Here, Pankhurst supporters march through Heptonstall.*

7. *Hebden Bridge in the 1890s. New top-and-bottom houses are being built on the upper-right hillside. In the centre is the high pitched roof of Hope Baptist chapel - which still struggles on. The valley of the river Hebden rises behind, leading up to Hardcastle Crags and Crimsworth. Heptonstall church is top left.*

8. *The railway brought the biggest social change. A print of Hebden Bridge station (1845), painted by A.F. Tait for a special series on the Manchester–Leeds line. Businesses abandoned the hillside water-driven mills. The station brought in coal and bales of cotton, and took out cheap trousers. The view was never quite so romantic as this. But Hebden Bridge was created.*

priests themselves were celibate (as they remain), unlike Anglican or Nonconformist ministers. They had little social contact with anyone outside their own congregation.

This sense of self-willed exclusion meant that, in Hebden, anyone who came from Luddenden Foot – downriver from Mytholmroyd, and at one time dominated by Murgatroyds' mill – was likely to be classed as one of 't'Foot Irish'. This is where many of those Irish incomers had settled. And when Hebden Bridge acquired a Roman Catholic church of its own, it was tucked away on a road which was rather cut off and lay, much of the day, in the shadow of the hill. Estate agents still call it the 'dark side' of town, and house prices are cheaper.

So what does 'local' mean, when you're talking about Hebden? By which I mean, in this book, the five civil parishes of Hebden Royd (Hebden Bridge and Mytholmroyd) in the valley and, on the uplands, Heptonstall, Erringden, Wadsworth and Blackshaw. In the 1980s, one sociological study of decay and revival in Hebden – a doctoral thesis by a Manchester-based researcher – concluded that the key date was 1971, the year of the decennial census. By then the 'invasion' had begun. But was not yet much more than a trickle. It reached full flood later in the 1970s. In charting attitudes, the researcher took 'local' to mean: anyone who came from a family which had lived in Hebden before that census date.

The Barker family were local on that definition, even though one story in the family is that, many years ago, we were Polish gypsies who'd come into Hull with the Baltic timber trade, and somehow acquired a Yorkshire name on their way to the upper Calder valley. It is certain that my great-great-grandfather was a bargee, whose son, grandson and great-grandson (my father) settled down in Mytholmroyd. It is also true that Barker men – including my father and his brothers – often had a slightly Slavic look. There is no other proof. Some have argued that there is a confusion here between the Polish city of Krakow and a North Yorkshire village called Cracoe. So be it.

The other definition of 'local' is: anyone who has a Greenwood or Sutcliffe in their family background. The merit of that definition, rather than an abrupt statistical cut-off date such as 1971, is that it reflects the movements of people and of history.

I'm happy with either definition. I fit into both of them. Both my parents came from local families. My father's father married a Greenwood. The genealogy of my mother's Ashworth father has been traced back through twelve generations. All were local. Among the forty-three surnames listed, there were five Greenwoods and four Sutcliffes. As names, Barker and Ashworth (eight of them on that same list) were already local enough for anyone.

My wife's father, James Huddleston, was a primary school headmaster in Hebden Bridge. He was born in Ulverston, Stan Laurel's Cumbrian home town. The youngest son in a large family, he went away to Leeds teacher training college. At the college, he met my future mother-in-law, Marion Ashworth. Her father, Will, was assistant to his father, Handley Ashworth, on the *Hebden Bridge Times*, and then succeeded him as editor. Marion's mother, Alice, was born in Heptonstall. After James's first teaching job in Halifax, he came to Hebden Bridge to take up his headship.

Taking account of all that, I think I can count as an honorary local, though I've lived away for years. Walking down the Champs Elysées, one dark winter's evening in Paris, I felt a huge wave of nostalgia. The speakers of a music shop were blasting out the *Messiah*. The localist anthem.

# 9. OUTSIDERS

The higher you go on these hillsides, the more the spirit of old Hebden is distilled. And perhaps the spirit of new Hebden, also. The former Co-op in one small hilltop village, Midgley, has just been re-opened as a 'community store'. The old store closed years ago. Without it, there was no shop left in the village. An uncle of mine was the Co-op manager in its last days. He was pleased to be invited to the re-opening. But 'they were all offcomers'. He only knew two people there.

'Offcomers' (or, some say, 'offcumden') is a strange word. As a child in Mytholmroyd or as a teenager in Hebden Bridge, I am sure I never heard it used. I do remember families or individuals being described as 'foreigners'. But this was said half-jokingly. It might mean Welsh or Irish, but it also included Geordies or Brummies. It could include people born in Halifax or Huddersfield. Or, even, sometimes, people born in a different village like Heptonstall or Blackshaw Head. Curiously, as I remember, it was seldom or never used of actual foreigners, like the postwar sprinkling of Poles or Ukrainians.

None of these outsiders or semi-outsiders was seen as any kind of threat. They fitted neatly into the existing social structure. They didn't arrive by the score, with a ready-made alternative ethos. From the 1960s new arrivals start to turn up, in large numbers, and armed with an ethos of their own. These arrivals were the *offcomers*. Oddly, I found that 'community' was a word seldom out of the new arrivals' conversation. But it was a kind of label, stuck over the reality of Us and Them.

Where did all these people come from? At the time, I put this question to Martin Parr in his Hebden Bridge house. He thought that they divided into groups, depending on the places they'd fled from. The main geographical sources were, he reckoned, Basingstoke in Hampshire, Leyland and Manchester in Lancashire, and Doncaster in the far West Riding. 'Word somehow gets around, and people come. Susie [his wife-to-be] and I are Manchester art school refugees.' Why was this? Because Manchester, before any inner-city regeneration, was a much grimmer place than it is now. Basingstoke and Leyland were both then being blitzed by an earlier, more ham-fisted version of top-down regeneration. Doncaster, once the proud capital of the coalfields (a title only challenged by Wakefield), was already beginning the downhill slide which, by now, means that half the social disaster stories in the press seem to happen in that town. Hebden's new arrivals were mostly in their late twenties or very early thirties.

In 1921, an official guide to Hebden Bridge could speak of it as 'the recognised centre in this country, if not the World, for the manufacture of fustian and corduroy cloths and garments.' More than thirty firms made corduroy which was 'shipped to every part of the globe'. The guide concluded: 'The town is a busy hive of industry, all the way from the breaking up of the cotton bale right on through spinning-mule, loom and dye vat, to the power-driven sewing machine.' Even in 1937, the official guide could say: 'The present industries of the area are many and varied.' (Hence the arrival of job seekers between the wars from other parts of Britain.) In the early 1970s, an official Department of Employment profile could still describe the 'general character' of Hebden as 'clothing and textile manufacturing, light engineering and machine tool manufacture, some poultry and egg production [though the biggest such business closed in 1972], agriculture, mostly small dairy farms.' And there was a scattering of other trades: baking, furniture, clog-making.

Within ten years almost all that had gone. The population of Hebden Bridge itself (leaving aside Mytholmroyd and the hill parishes) was 4,778 in 1881. Twenty years later, in 1901, it had risen to 7,536. This was the top mark. From there until the 1971 census, the graph was downhill all the way. During those seventy years, the England and Wales population rose by 45 per cent. In Hebden Bridge it *fell* by 44 per cent. It had dropped by 20 per cent in the two decades 1951–71. Unemployment remained low, but only because younger people left, and more and more of the remaining population had retired. Much of the housing was out-of-date. For example, nationally, according to that census, 83 per cent of households had their own bath or shower, an inside lavatory and hot water. In Hebden Bridge the figure was 64 per cent. Many homes were rented from private landlords.

A cloud of gloom started to settle. As early as 1966, the local MP, Douglas Houghton, spoke of an 'atmosphere of stagnation and decline, which simply must be arrested'. A letter in the *Hebden Bridge Times* spoke of the town as 'a dirty, scruffy hole'. The main street of Heptonstall had empty houses and even broken windows. The strongest symbol of what was happening was the winding-up of Hebden Bridge Cooperative Society. The upper Calder valley had been among the earliest pioneers of the Co-op. The Hebden Bridge society was founded soon after the Rochdale pioneers' 1844 launch. The Co-op's head office and hall was by far the biggest building in the centre of Hebden Bridge. The society went from a trading profit of £17,000 in 1951 to a loss of £10,626 in 1967. The will to continue had gone. The managing secretary was sent to prison for embezzlement.

In all the surrounding districts there were separate little cooperative societies. In Mytholmroyd, for example, the store – with the beehive trademark carved on the front and the motto 'Man Know Thyself' – was the heart of the village. I was given a rainbow badge to mark its 1947 centenary. This Co-op, also, shut. The main building is now converted into flats, with the inaccurate, semi-literate name of Coiners Wharfe.

What to do? The main thinking came from the Calder Civic Trust which had been founded in May 1965 – in opposition to the threats to Hardcastle Crags – by David Fletcher. He was a local-born teacher who became head of environmental studies at Manchester Polytechnic. In a document he co-authored in 1972, he laid out the three Rs for Hebden's future: 'Retention of existing industry; limited residential development; realisation of recreational potential.' He also thought Hebden could become 'a site for new small businesses the new population would want to set up', creating 'a virtuous, self-reinforcing spiral of recovery'. He went on to found Pennine Heritage, as a vigorous, wider-based campaign group. The word spread. Research shows that by 1981 things in Hebden were already changing for the better. Today there are reported to be more than 500 firms paying business rates in the HX7 postal district, which covers Hebden Bridge, Mytholmroyd and the hillsides. The streets of Hebden Bridge are awash with cafés, full of weekend visitors. Coaches for tour parties park up by the railway station.

This economic turn-round hasn't yet brought much change in the numbers of people. By the 2001 census – the latest breakdown of such local statistics – the population had ceased falling and the age spread was more like the national average: more young people, fewer elderly. But the population of Hebden Bridge itself was still only 4,121 (that is, fewer than in 1881). In the 2001 census, the population of the entire Hebden district came to 13,125. Mytholmroyd accounted for 4,135 of that total. The rest lived mostly in the hillside hamlets and small villages.

When the statisticians release updated local figures from the 2011 census, all these totals may shade upwards: new houses have been shoe-horned in; and large old buildings (mills, warehouses, chapels, pubs) have been converted into flats. The hilltops, which had been in a state of total flight and collapse, have flourished in a way which was never expected. Internet connection has helped. Most important everywhere was a change in occupation and class, especially among the hill dwellers. Many of these are now, in census language, 'professional and managerial'.

Far more workpeople from Hebden now commute out than was ever the case in the past. And many more now commute in. In Mytholmroyd, two lawyers decided they had had enough of the big-office life. They set up an information service for the legal profession. They kept their subscribers up to date on changes in the law, and publicised leading cases. Their business became one of the largest local employers. In due course, it was bought out by the long-established law publishers Sweet & Maxwell, who themselves have since been bought out by the international firm Thomson Reuter. The general Hebden dress style is now casual in the extreme. But I am told: 'Watch the trains that get in at Mytholmroyd station around nine in the morning, and you'll see a flood of lawyers in suits, arriving.'

Local initiatives like this law firm are the essential components of a true economic revival. But takeovers change the game. At Mytholmroyd, Thomson Reuter now employs more than 200 people. But the company announces job cuts as I write this. And if it decides it wants to switch sites, either within Britain or even to Bombay . . .

Hebden's other large employer is a firm called Calrec, which makes audio equipment. Again this was started by a small group of local people. Calrec is now based in the old Nutclough mill, which Pennine Heritage helped to preserve from demolition, partly because of its importance in the Hebden townscape and partly because of its history as a workers' cooperative. Calrec employs about 160 people. But it, too, has now been bought out – by a Japanese company.

Faced with a dismal future, most of the local politicians had in the early 1960s decided to go for the standard solution of the day: a central area redevelopment plan. They went ahead with demolitions. Two entire sets of streets had been demolished by the end of the 1950s: streets which, in Hebden terms, counted as slums. Between 1962 and 1966, more than 100 further houses were emptied or demolished, and nearly 200 others were scheduled for clearance as 'unfit for human habitation'. This description included nearly all the top-and-bottom houses that gave the townscape its character. David Fletcher's Calder Civic Trust started to preach conservation: 'People will not come to live here unless it is a nice place.'

Fortunately, the planners appointed to reshape Hebden took years to come up with their plan, and little of it was carried out. In the meantime, the value of many houses dropped to almost zero. Hebden started to reap the benefit of planning blight. The market does work. There is always a price at which anything will sell. And Birchcliffe, an important segment of the Hebden Bridge townscape, gained government designation as one of the country's first 'general improvement areas'. Conservation was starting to win the battle, though it took another five years before a government minister would state: 'We have pensioned off the bulldozer.'

Hebden was one of the places that led the way. Partly it was due to local initiatives. But partly it was due to a useful *lack* of initiative. In those years, the towns and cities which wrecked their prospects for the future were those who thought themselves to be 100 per cent get-up-and-go. They pointed bulldozers at all signs of the past like a hawker setting his bird at its quarry. Bradford, for example, destroyed much of its Victorian heritage. Liverpool's streetscape suffered more from postwar development than from the Luftwaffe. By contrast, Manchester and Leeds left their city centres largely alone (though there had been schemes to demolish almost everything), while destroying many of the streets all around the centre. In the long run, doziness paid off.

And so it was with Hebden. But the havering and the uncertainty, and the wish to bring back a moribund industrial past, meant that that influx of change – and especially the influx of new people – came as an even greater shock than it might otherwise have been. Some locals might see the newcomers as 'fresh blood'. But a 1980 survey found that many others saw them as 'the hairy community', 'hippie type' or 'non-productive'. Small towns and villages are unforgiving places.

The changes were striking. The 1980 survey found that three-quarters of the earlier residents worked locally or very near by. Only half of the new people were so close to their work. Commuting to Manchester was especially strong. The railway, which once brought in cotton and took away boxes of fustian or corduroy trousers, now shifted commuters. The newcomers earned half as much again as the locals. They spent less in Hebden as a proportion of their income. But, of course, their incomes were higher, so they spent at least as much in cash terms. By 1980, Hebden had caught up with the national figures for baths or showers, inside lavatories and hot water systems. In ten years owner-occupation rose from 50 per cent to 71 per cent (the national figure was then only 56 per cent).

What did the newcomers say they liked about the place, in the 1980 survey? In this order: the countryside, the people and the access. Hebden Bridge had 'character': 'It's a grand town'; 'It is a confident place'; 'It is a thriving, living place with a real north country atmosphere of its own.' And what did they dislike? 'The surrounding hills make you feel as if you are living in a goldfish bowl', or 'The place is becoming fossilised, all tourism, antiques and high house prices.' And were the newcomers committed to Hebden? Almost threequarters of the locals expected to be still living here in ten years' time, but fewer than half of the newcomers.

A 1979 study of rural recovery or decay, carried out at the University of Exeter by Anne Glyn-Jones, confirmed that, for an economic turn-round, 'there may simply be no substitute for local leadership and initiative'. Hebden demonstrates this. But did anyone realise it would lead, in the end, to a shop called Cabbages and Cushions, local stockists of Farrow & Ball – the smartest of all providers of paint to the upper bourgeoisie?

# 10. TEMPERANCE

Tom Morgan used to put on 35mm film screenings in a back room at Zion chapel. He bought the projector second-hand from the first Hebden Bridge cinema ('Jack Shaw's wood hut'). It was at Tom's shows that I first saw early Chaplin, then still unrivalled as a screen comedian. Here, also, I saw the silent version of Arthur Conan Doyle's *The Lost World* (1925), with Wallace Beery as an intrepid Professor Challenger, confronting the mysteriously surviving dinosaurs. When Steven Spielberg's *Jurassic Park* – roughly the same story – was released in 1993, I wasn't the only person in the audience who thought that the old stop-motion Plasticene monsters were as good as, or better than, the computer-generated updatings. This wasn't pure nostalgia: the earlier film was restored, remastered and rescreened in 2001.

The Morgan family ran Zion chapel: especially old Sam, Tom's father, and Tom's brother Maurice. Sam was the boss at Zion in between working as office manager and 'the power behind the throne' at the local clog factory. This mill, too, is now empty and awaiting conversion into, probably, 'luxury flats'. You used to walk past it, with its stacks of timber left out to season, if you went by foot from Mytholmroyd to Hebden Bridge. At the fringe of Hebden Bridge you reached the council-run gasworks. Parents took you that way on purpose, if you were starting to get better from a bad chest-cold, in order to inhale the supposedly germ-killing fumes. It wasn't until the gas works closed that I realised why the trees above it, in Crow Nest wood, never had any grass or bracken under them. It was no surprise that the fumes also caused germs to wilt. Now, hey presto, the earth is green again.

You look out across to Crow Nest from the old Mayroyd mill. This was originally called Barker mill. It was named after William Barker, to whom I suspect I'm very distantly related. He was the first wholesale clothier in Hebden Bridge. In the 1850s, he added a sewing shop to his dyeing-and-finishing corduroy and fustian business. His wife and daughters were the first seamstresses. For years, a high stone doorway at Mayroyd mill was still known as 'Barker's Arch'. It was especially popular, I was told, among 'courting couples'. The old mill has now been prettily converted into houses. Nicola Jones, of the new Calder Civic Trust, lives in one of them.

Tom Morgan saw me in 1978 in the sheltered flats he'd retired to. Both his father and his brother were lay preachers ('they could baptise and bury, but not marry'). At eighty, Tom was tall and thin and keen-faced. He was interested in everything we talked about. He trained as a mechanic and worked at jobs all over the country. It turned out that showing the films was only part of his general passion for photography. His old magic lantern slides were under the bed in his little flat.

He was born in Mytholmroyd, in cottages that had since been pulled down. 'I can show thee a photo on it.' His other photographs included a fire at Thornber's hatcheries. No one wanted to miss a fire. He found pictures of other factories aflame. He and I talked of the vanished mills. Here was a photo of the Redacre dye house, now gone. Here was an old sepia photo of the Cragg Vale mills – Tom called it 'Turvin valley'. It was from before his time, but he remembered the last mill in Cragg being pulled down for its stone. Hawksclough mill was another he saw pulled down. A sepia photo showed the crowds watching another chimney-stack toppled.

The annual Mytholmroyd 'demonstrations' – that is, galas – for charity were big events. The funds were split between the Halifax pre-NHS infirmary and a nurses' centre at Mytholmroyd. 'Yer grand-fayther might be on this,' Tom said, showing me one of his own photos, and he may have been right. My grandfather's lapel badge as demonstration steward is one of the family mementoes I inherited. It is in a cardboard box five feet to my left as I write.

The chapels, whether Primitives or Wesleyans, ran the demonstrations. The parade, 'wi' a float on to tek childer', ended up at

White House Fields: 'Juggling, boxing, races, tug o' wahr, harriers.' Robertshaw's Westfield mill had a tug of war team. Here, definitely, was a photograph of my grandfather, perhaps from his days as a tackler at that mill.

Most of the officials at the chapels were men – but the women ran the men. Sam was the chapel secretary at the Primitives. But Tom said Sam was answerable to 'Mrs Charnley, Mrs Boocock, Mrs Gibson, Mrs Dakin, her sister Annie and Mrs Johnson'. The Primitives kept up the old passion for open-air 'camp meetings', a 'sing' and a 'love feast'. This pre-empted the contemporary passion for shaking hands with the next person in a congregation. 'Rattifer' (ratafia) biscuits were handed round, along with a two-handled cup.

Whitsuntide always seemed, to me, to be a bigger deal than Easter. (In Hebden, as in Scotland, Good Friday was a working day.) At Whit, the chapel gave a party for children, with plenty of 'school buns' – a lovely, sticky, currant-laden bread. At the beginning of May there was the Spa Sunday walk (pronounced Spaw) up Cragg Vale to where a little spring came out of the hillside. This was supposed to be good for your health. Water from the spring, or at other times water from the tap, was shaken up in a bottle with hard lumps of black liquorice. We called it 'spa water'. It had a sulphurous taste.

'Chapel were t'centre of the universe, then.' Tom asked me if I was in the nativity plays. I said I was: you were drafted. Later, at my Hebden Bridge chapel, I even came on stage in a Sunday school minstrel show, my face blackened with cork, beneath a wig that waggled its topknot when I pulled a string, and sang 'The Camptown Races'. Chorus: 'Doodah, doodah, day.'

The Morgan family – to all appearances as local as anyone could be, but Welsh by name – came from Wellington in Shropshire to work at a mill in Mytholmroyd. The mill's boss was a Wesleyan, but Sam Morgan switched to the Primitives. This was the kind of chapel he'd been to in Shropshire. The congregations loved to give testimony extempore. During one testimony, Tom said, the speaker called out, 'Look ye to the Lord'. A voice from the back responded, 'I'm looking, Joshua!'

The Band of Hope, where you pledged never to drink, was omnipresent. Young men went to Sunday school, often until their twenties.

'The message were, the "white man" is "a slave" to drink,' Tom said. He still remembered the songs: 'Father, dear father, come home with me now,/The clock in the steeple strikes one.' My father signed the pledge at this same chapel. Drink was one of the demarcation lines between the rough and respectable working classes. Long after that pledge, I don't remember my father drinking anything stronger than a pint of mild and bitter. There was never any drink in the house.

Tom trained as a mechanic through an apprenticeship at a small engineering firm in Bridge mill, in the middle of Hebden Bridge. In launching his campaign for renovation, rather than demolition, this mill became David Fletcher's first focus. A corn mill had been established here about 700 years ago. By the 1960s, the building, with its stubby chimney, was standing empty and was scheduled to be pulled down. He set about restoring it. Having previously built his own house, he did much of the work on Bridge mill himself. It now has one of the very few mill chimneys left, locally – half a dozen at most.

Tom was born on 28 June 1897. He went to the Burnley Road 'bo-erd scho-il' till he was thirteen, and started work on 1 July 1910. He didn't switch to part-time work at eleven, as many boys then did. But he had half-days at a woodwork centre in Hebden Bridge. Decades later, this was precisely where I spent hours chiselling out a matchbox holder and a photograph frame, as part of the grammar school course. I still have the photo frame, now rather wobbly. I don't know what happened to the matchbox holder.

In Hebden, as Tom saw it, there were 'the upper ten, of course, but they weren't snobbish'. There was, also – as Jonas Brown said – little deference. 'Joe Thomas, at Hangingroyd dye works, would muck in with the dyeing. You couldn't tell t'boss from t'worker. Some of 'em were as hard-working as t'men.'

In the First World War, Tom went to work at a factory in York. In the Second World War, he was drafted to a shipbuilder's in Birkenhead. What he mainly remembered from those years of shipbuilding were the demarcation disputes. 'You ended up tekking two and a half days over a ten minute job.' Hebden was never a strong union place. Tom belonged to the engineering union, the AEU, but he never paid the political levy.

When they erected a First World War memorial at Mytholmroyd, with a statue of a Tommy in puttees, a Morgan presided, and the Hebden Bridge brass band played. In more recent years, the statue was vandalised. The soldier's rifle was repeatedly stolen. Even the head was knocked off.

By the early years of the twenty-first century – perhaps because the British government had decided to plunge into yet more wars – the memorial was seen as a public disgrace. It was repaired and laid out afresh. My uncle Leslie, who had married my aunt Marjorie at Zion chapel, cut the ribbon. He had been at the D-Day landing in a ship on which many of his fellow-soldiers were killed by a direct hit. The bodies were thrown into the sea.

# II. BROTHERHOOD

The Hebden Bridge brass band still flourishes. There have been years when it almost packed it in. So far, it has always pulled through. I was briefly a member when I was at primary school. I caught the bus to Hebden Bridge with my cornet. I was never any good, and I found it all very laborious. The highest point I reached was to sit on the back row as we played on a bandstand in a Halifax park. I could barely follow the music, even for 'Bless this House', which was my constant practice piece.

I struck a deal with my parents. If I passed the eleven-plus exam to go to grammar school, could I give up the cornet? They agreed. I did pass, no doubt helped by this motivating bargain. You could say that this cornet changed my life. Such locally linked music has indelible charms. Handel wrote the *Messiah* as an Easter oratorio, but in Yorkshire chapels it was sung at Christmas. I still try to hear the *Messiah* every Christmas. The brassier the better.

I thought that the band might be one way to contrast the new and old populations of Hebden, with the band membership as representative of the old. I get the telephone number of the band president, Alan Bottomley, from the tourist office. He is a retired bank manager. Tonight, he says, is band practice night. Would I like to come along? We arrange to meet outside the library at Mytholmroyd where I spent many hours in my childhood (as I did, later, at Hebden Bridge library).

The library faces a patch of grass where cottages were slum-cleared in the years before the Second World War. One of them was where my mother and father opened their first fish and chip shop. When this cottage was demolished, the fish and chip shop moved to a building near the railway station – now a 'desirable home'. This is where my own first memory of the shop dates from. Errand-runners from the nearby mills came in with vast orders for fish and chips, or fishcake and chips, or sometimes just chips 'with scraps'. (Glossary: A fishcake here meant a sliver of fish between two slices of potato, all fried together. Scraps were the bits of batter that fell off during frying.) I was only once allowed to pull the handle of the lethally sharp potato slicer. The shop was a great success.

This grass outside the library is where I got my first, slightly bizarre taste of party politics. John Belcher, an obscure junior trade minister in Clement Attlee's postwar Labour government, was the local MP. In 1948, a public tribunal found him guilty of accepting some modest bribes from a racketeer called Sidney Stanley. The wartime system of rationing – food, clothes, furniture, petrol – was being carried on, regardless, as 'socialist planning.' The pressures to dodge government controls, and dip into black-marketeering, were extreme.

The fixers were called spivs. They were usually figures of fun (as they were in BBC TV's *Dad's Army*). But almost everyone made some use of 'under-the-counter' skills. The case of John Belcher turned on the government's controls over paper – could a football pools firm lay hands on some more? – and, almost laughably, on the rules about the import of American pinball machines. Sidney Stanley, alias Solomon Koszyski, alias Stanley Rechtand, alias Schlomo ben Chaim, was a Polish-born professional fraudster and all-purpose fixer.

Stanley fled to the newly established state of Israel in 1949, and never came back to be prosecuted. He gave a long newspaper interview to the then-bestselling *People* newspaper about his cleverness in getting away. Belcher, a former railway clerk, quietly resigned his seat.

The by-election hustings I trotted along to was held on top of a solid brickwork (and never used) air-raid shelter, built at the edge of the patch of grass. Douglas Houghton was Belcher's would-be successor as Labour MP. He was known locally only as the man who broadcast regular home hints on the BBC's Home Service (the forerunner of Radio 4). Though the Attlee government was already in deep financial trouble, Houghton promised that an era of fairness to all would continue into the far future. He was elected, and was for many years a well-liked local figure. Belcher went back to a railway job.

Alan Bottomley's car draws up outside the library. For all my knowledge of Mytholmroyd, he thinks I'll never find the rehearsal room on my own. He is right. Off to one side of the Cragg Vale road, with Bell Hole in the far distance, there is an electronic gate into the grounds of a private nursery school, and beyond that a business park. This is where Thornber's had their chicken hatchery.

Ralph Thornber, grandson of the founder of the firm, lives in a large converted farmhouse a bit further up the hill. (His name is pronounced Raif, which his mother preferred. His father, now dead, preferred the more northerly pronunciation, Ralf.) Ralph's daughter had the idea for the nursery school, which many parents now flock to. The nursery is also the key, according to Ralph, which unlocked the local planners' objections to rebuilding the old chicken huts as lettable premises for firms. The replacement sheds are surrounded by greenery. The business park, and Ralph's other conversions of older property in Mytholmroyd, are now big employers. They include Mumtaz, a well-known manufacturer of Indian food.

That afternoon, before I go up to see the band, I look around the small graveyard behind the Wesleyan Methodist church at Mytholmroyd. This is where I was first thought old enough to go to a funeral – for my uncle Harry Barker. Harry was 'a bit backward', as they said then – that is, brain-damaged. He worked as a handyman in a local Mytholmroyd bakers until all such small firms were bought out and closed down by Garfield Weston's Allied Bakeries, the inventors of Mother's Pride sliced bread.

Harry lies here in the same grave as his mother Elizabeth (Libby) and his father Tom. (My grandmother Barker died before I could really know her.) In a similar unostentatious plot, a few feet away, I notice the grave of the Thornber firm's founder, Edgar. He had launched into the hatchery business in the middle of a big fustian workers' strike in 1906–9, which meant he was laid off. He turned what had been a hobby into a vast business, which his son Cyril, Ralph's father, took over after his father died.

For years, jobs at Thornber's buoyed up the Hebden economy. Then, like so many other local firms, it too was killed off. The cause the firm gave was 'foreign competition'. But, talking to Cyril, years back,

I thought it was also that he began to see himself as an academic. He was making up for the college years he never had. His father took him straight from school into the hatchery business. As head of the firm from 1944, Cyril employed a squad of geneticists, and took pride in the details of new breeds. Less subtle firms – especially those in America, with its larger domestic market – could do the job cheaper.

For Cyril's father, Edgar, the business was everything. Admittedly, he built a big house, where, living as a child in our nearby council house, I once went to a garden party. (Edgar's business partner, Ben Stansfield, had married a cousin of my mother's: the usual Hebden story of interconnections.) But Cyril told me that his father's greatest pleasure, away from work, was tending the garden and having old friends round to play snooker. In his photographs, Edgar Thornber could be first cousin to the car maker William Morris, later Lord Nuffield. Their look is, at the same time, both determined and self-effacing – one of them a former shuttlemaker, the other a former bike mechanic. Life stories out of H.G. Wells.

It's through Ralph Thornber's beneficence that the brass band has a home in the business park. For years the players had continued to practise in the same space at Hebden Bridge where, long ago, I'd tentatively joined in. Downstairs, later, in the same building, my mother went to local history classes. Suddenly Calderdale borough council sold the building to a developer, without giving anyone else a chance to buy it. When the brass band struggled to find a good alternative, Ralph said, 'Let me know. I'll see you right.' And he did. The band is now at chicken shed 1(a). 'It's £5,000 a year,' says Alan Bottomley, 'and for that we can play when we want to. All night, it could be.' It was the neighbours' fear of noise that made a place so hard to find.

The band is full of zest. It has worked its way up, over recent years, into the top class of the brass band league, the Championship Section. Alan tells me: 'Six years ago, we were at the bottom. We couldn't mount a concert. We had to pay people to come. We had to beseech them. Now they come knocking at the door.' Soon the band will face playing against classic opponents like Brighouse & Rastrick and Fodens, rivals from the previous glory decades.

Players, both men and women, are starting to come in for tonight's rehearsal. Shelves hold championship cups and shields from the heroic past. A few months before, the band appointed a new music director: Roy Curran, who used to play in the Birmingham symphony orchestra. We shake hands. Behind us, the industrial cacophony of tuning-up begins. Holding his baton, Roy begins to comment on the band's previous performance. 'The hymn tune was excellent, but the march was loose.' He is thin and a little stooped. He looks to be in his sixties, at least. But, as he talks, in a quiet but precise Brummie accent, he has what I assume is the right manner for a good conductor: he is courteous, but also firm and honest. Ian Coleman, on E-flat bass, has written an orchestration, 'It's Madness', based on three songs by the pop group of the same name. Roy guides the band through it. 'Let's have a bit more oompah, shall we?'

I sit at the back. One of the black, upturned instrument cases beside me has two badges on it: Butlin's Brass Band Festival Skegness 2010, and Mineworkers Open National.

The set-up is very democratic. 'We don't sack players,' Alan tells me. 'One trombone player, for example, realised he wasn't up to it as the band got better. Usually, it's just the grapevine that does the job.' Or there are other pressures. The present first cornet, still at college in Manchester, is about to go off to Black Dyke. 'We're not big enough or rich enough to compete at that level. But if we're stuck for a player, we can usually get someone. Some players get fed up with Black Dyke, which is a kind of dictatorship. Black Dyke is *the* band, even though they don't win every championship every year. All the same, players pay to come to sit here at Hebden.'

Who are they, these sixteen men and nine women? They are a varied bunch. Ian Coleman is a bus driver, who lives in the upper Calder valley, though not in Hebden. Two of the players are still at Calder High School, two or three are at college. Among the rest are a doctor, a dentist, a micro-biologist, a hospital technician and an electrician. Ages range from sixteen to fifty. Some travel many miles to come to the practice evenings.

My original hypothesis doesn't stand up. The players are patriotic about being the Hebden Bridge band, and are conscious of its great history. But they are a community of shared interest, not a geographical community, and few were born or bred locally. Here, no valid points can be made about 'locals' versus 'offcomers'. The band's existence is a sign of *both* change *and* continuity. The band has more than 2,000 pieces of music on file, going back to 1901. 'They would be £60 a set,' I'm told. In 1901, almost all the band would be working men from local mills. Not any more. But the band itself, as an entity, *is* local.

'It's a lifelong hobby,' Alan Bottomley says. 'It's a brotherhood.' He plays no instrument himself, but as a child he would 'nip over the wall to hear bands playing in the park grandstand'. Family is an important ingredient in the glue that holds brass-banding together. 'It's a family affair,' Alan confirms. In the present band, he checks it out: 'A husband, wife and two sons, a father and son, an uncle and nephew, a husband and wife, and another husband and wife.' Ian Coleman followed his father into the band.

The rehearsal carries on as Alan and I drive back down for me to pick up my car. 'You have to have an absolute commitment,' he says. 'The show goes on. If you accept an invitation to give a concert, you have to do it, come what may.'

I have to pursue 'localism' elsewhere. As I interview Lesley Jones in 2010, she is one of the two members of the Hebden Royd town council who can claim to be local, in the usual sense. Her mother and father were in the armed forces, and moved around a lot. She was born in Dover, but came to the Calder valley because of her mother's local ties: Lesley's grandmother kept a stall in Halifax borough market. Lesley grew up in Hebden – living, at first, on Dodnaze, the same hilltop council estate as Christine Jackson. 'It was wonderful. We hardly ever went down the hill, except for school.' She has now lived for ten years in her semi-detached house above the Hebden Bridge railway station. Her husband comes in as we talk. He is just back from the nearby smallholding he inherited from his mother.

Lesley is in her late fifties now, welcoming and cheerful. Now deputy mayor, she is trying to decide whether or not to stand for election again in 2011. (In the end, she decides to.) 'I'm in the council,' she says, 'because of a complete inability to say no'. There are piles of council papers on a table. But she does feel that her voice is important. She speaks about a friend who feels that 'locals are intimidated by the new people who take over committees'. She says: 'They are not so outgoing or so used to presenting their arguments in a highly rational way. It's a vicious circle. Those who do, do. I wish more locals would get involved. I would like to get more of them to speak up for themselves. You can't bring back the past.'

'In the 1970s,' she says, 'the town was dead. If it hadn't been saved by the hippies, it wouldn't be the same Hebden Bridge.' Even so, Lesley thinks the proportion of newcomers in Hebden 'has reached saturation point'. House prices drive the younger families out – perhaps only to other, cheaper parts of the Calder valley – and they find they can't get back. At school, Lesley joined the Civic Trust in its early days. But now she wonders if the trust hasn't 'tipped the balance the wrong way, just making the place good for tourists'.

The Hebden Royd town hall has just been bought by a 'community trust', which was angered by the way the old band building was sold off to developers. When David Cameron made one of his speeches, as Prime Minister, about the 'Big Society', one television report took this initiative as an example of what he meant. This Hebden trust decided to bid for the picture house next. I wander into the town hall. I'm pleased to see in the hallway the old brass plaque, thick with metal polish, which commemorates the two local men who were killed in the Boer War and the three who died there of disease.

The town council has just renamed one of its meeting rooms in honour of Joseph Greenwood, a local pioneer of the nineteenth-century cooperative movement. He ran the Nutclough worker cooperative, in the mill now occupied by Calrec. Talking to the 2010–11 mayor (a Labour man) about Joseph Greenwood, I get the impression that the Boer War is of less interest. Some bits of Hebden's past dovetail into a narrative – a party line? – about Hebden's past. But parts do not.

In the 2011 Hebden Royd elections, Lesley Jones – who's been looking forward to, and deserves, a year as mayor – is knocked out of her town council seat. She has run as a genuine, hard-working independent. She loses because, in the party interest, Labour has put up a full slate of its own candidates in her three-seat ward. One of the very rare local voices on the council is lost. Talk of 'community' can be a thin veneer.

# 12. WAR

Edmund Ashworth has no memorial in his name in Hebden that I know of. But my mother-in-law, Marion, used to talk about her favourite uncle Edmund, who had been killed in the First World War. When she died, aged ninety-three, one of the old photographs Sally and I brought away from her cold Hebden Bridge cottage, after the funeral, was a picture of Edmund in uniform. New bouts of nostalgia have broken out, for almost any British war, except the ones we have recently been fighting. But we didn't know that this photograph would start us on a kind of quest.

There was also a picture of Edmund's brother Will, in the uniform he wore as one of the Hebden Bridge Ambulance Volunteers in the Boer War. Will had sent back reports on that war to the *Hebden Bridge Times*. We already had a 134-page book, reprinting his reports from when he set sail in June 1899 to his return in December 1900. Will gave the little book to Sally, as his granddaughter, in June 1943. The tone is that of a fair-minded, honest reporter. He describes, for example, the record of the Boers' highly accurate Mauser guns. Provided the Mausers' bullet tips hadn't been scored across to make devastating wounds, they were apparently seen – by both Will and the infantry – as 'more merciful' than the ammunition used by the British riflemen. As eventual editor of the paper, Will's best-known trainee was Bernard Ingham, who became Margaret Thatcher's Prime Ministerial press secretary and general bulldog.

Sally and I knew very little about Edmund Ashworth, except that he was in his late twenties when he was killed in Flanders. But we did know that, young as he was, he had had more of a life than many of the war dead. Until he volunteered for the army, he had been a teacher in Halifax.

In the late 1930s, when my brother-in-law was enrolled as a pupil at the same junior school, his great-uncle Edmund's photograph was on the wall of the assembly hall, as a local hero.

Sally and I had decided to take up a special Eurotunnel offer, partly in order to see a Goya exhibition at Lille, and partly to drift around all those places in Picardy we usually drove past on our way to some sun in the south. I wanted to visit Lutyens's great memorial at Thiepval in northern France, which I had only seen in photographs. I'd never been to any war cemetery before. I couldn't quite understand why nostalgia for unbearable pain should infect the British so many decades later.

If Thiepval, why not also a cemetery where we had some connection, however slender? But where was Edmund Ashworth, one of Hebden's local heroes, buried? All we knew was that his parents had been out to visit the grave, once, after the war. No one else we knew of had ever been. A few days before we set off, I looked up the phone number of the Commonwealth War Graves Commission. This turned out to be the most efficient public body in Britain I've ever had dealings with. I was impressed, but I don't like to think what the moral is.

I got through at the second attempt. No bleeping set of pre-recorded options. The operator asked what the initial of the last name was and put me straight through. What was the full surname? 'Ashworth.' First name? 'Edmund.' Any other information? 'He lived near Halifax, so he probably joined the Duke of Wellington's. They had their barracks there.'

A slight pause and then: 'Lance-Corporal Edmund Lord Ashworth, son of Handley and Alice Ashworth of 4 Sandy Gate, Hebden Bridge. [A house I used to go to when I was walking out with Sally.] Died 13th December 1915, aged twenty-nine. He was in the 1st/4th battalion of the Duke of Wellington's West Riding Regiment. He is buried at the Talana Farm cemetery, near Ypres: plot III, row D, grave No. 1.'

By the next post a route guide arrived, with some history of the cemetery. It was begun in April 1915 by Zouaves – that is, Algerians in the French army. Like some other front-line farmhouses, it was given its name by the British from an episode in the Boer War. Perhaps the flat Flanders landscape had echoes of the veldt for NCOs who – like Edmund's ambulanceman brother Will – had been in South Africa only a few years before. That, too, had been a war in which Kitchener was a leading figure – as he was in the First World War until his death in a torpedoed ship in 1916 – and where territory so laboriously won by men in trenches was fenced off behind barbed wire.

So we had to go to Ypres. The fields were glazed with snow. Near Hazebrouck, we saw a sign and swung off the motorway. The villages we passed were small and crushingly dull. Very different from the Hebden 'Fustianopolis' in its heyday, where Edmund Ashworth grew up. Nothing looks as closed down as French provincial life. One little road had two dreary glass-sided sheds, with barrier poles pointing up to the sky. This was the frontier. We were in Belgium.

Before long, we could see the spire of Ypres cathedral. This view was as pretty as a postcard. At the edge of Ypres we followed the commission's instructions. Find the railway station. Take a series of lefts and rights till you reach Diksmuidseweg. Then drive in the direction of Boezinge. I was beginning to feel anxious, even slightly ill – like before a funeral.

The road was built up into a causeway, like driving through the Fens. There were no hedges or other field barriers. Here, somewhere, was the Yser canal. For most of the war, the Germans were on the east of it, and we – I automatically think of 'we' – were mainly on the west. But a bulge of Allied territory, the Ypres salient, spread across the canal. Talana Farm was about one mile from the front line. We went slowly. On the left I saw a clean white wall, slightly below the road. This must be the first cemetery we were told to look out for. Then, about 200 yards away, across a field, we saw another plain white wall with a little classical entrance. This must be Talana Farm cemetery, though there was no sign to say so. We got out and saw, between the fields, a clear green walk. The fields were full of twisted black stalks about a foot high. They looked like charred crucifixes.

We walked up to the cemetery and in through the brick porch. There were 529 graves in the usual neat rows. The identical shapes and sizes created a surreal effect. At the far corner from where we came in was a tall white cross. The cemetery was on a slight slope. Plot III was just above us. We walked up among the gravestones. Most of them had a little shrub at the foot. Gunner W.H. Whatton, who died in September 1917, had a wreath of fabric poppies with a hand-written note: 'Thinking of you often. Love from all the family. Rest in peace.' I noticed a Corporal Trewartha, presumably related to the Trewartha my father played crown bowls with. Plots III and IV had many graves of the Duke of Wellington's Regiment.

We found row D first of all. We went along through the snow. Here was grave No. 1. It was under a small tree which looked as if it might have been planted after the Second World War. The tree was leafless now, but it had made Edmund Ashworth's stone greener, and harder to read, than the others. The green reminded me of the stones in Hebden graveyards, which are always thick with lichen. The stone gave only the regimental details and below – barely visible through the green – were the words: 'At Rest.' I assumed that this phrase was chosen by his parents from the selection the commission permitted. Absolute stoicism. Corporal Trewartha's stone said: 'Until Day Breaks and the Shadows Flee Away.' Nearby, Private Sykes – a very West Yorkshire name – had: 'Thy Will Be Done.'

Both Sally and I found it strange to be here. After all, Edmund Ashworth was someone we'd never met, only heard about, and seen in a photograph. We knew almost nothing about his life or his death. I felt an odd mixture of abstraction and overwhelming sadness. I didn't think this related directly to Edmund Ashworth. It was the emotion produced by the cemetery on this cold, clear, inappropriately beautiful day.

We took snapshots, feeling like out-of-place tourists. We knew we would never come back. Sally said she wished that her mother, Marion, could have known that we'd come. Her mother came from a family unusually small for those days. Marion was an only child and an only niece. She was ten when Edmund died.

I had thought that we would want to stay and look around. Emotionally it was too much. I noticed, as we went back down the slope, that some graves were set closer together, in pairs or trios. These soldiers must have been killed together, and no one knew which limb is which. Some graves said: 'Known to be Buried Here', or 'Believed to be Buried Here', or 'Buried Near this Spot'. The porch had a little metal door in one wall. A niche behind it had a list of the dead and a visitors' book. We signed our names, and left. We walked back down the fields, through the blackened stumps, saying nothing.

We drove into Ypres and parked in the gloomy square next to the Cloth Hall, rebuilt in replica after being shelled almost flat. (In old wartime photos, the remains of the tower stick up like three broken fingers.) We ate sticky Belgian cakes. A waitress told us the shortest way to Lille. We went past signs that showed us where the front line was in 1917, 1916 and 1915. They were only hundreds of yards apart. On each side were signposts to war cemetery after war cemetery. We realised we were on the Menin Road, one of the great killing fields of the Flanders front.

From Lille we set off towards Thiepval, through what had once been France's greatest coal mining district. Soon we could see the top of the Thiepval memorial, across miles of frozen fields. I couldn't get the memory of Talana Farm out of my mind. When we reached Thiepval, we were like insects next to Lutyens's 150-foot-high memorial arch. We went up twenty-five shallow steps, into the middle of the arch. The walls were lined with the names of the 73,367 British soldiers who died on the Somme and had no known grave. On the Somme, as near Ypres, many were just blown to bits. The sheer numbers of the dead drove home the anonymity and futility of that war in a way that Edmund Ashworth's grave could never do. There, at least, one man was buried, and remembered, as an individual.

I saw a small metal door like the one at Talana Farm. Another visitors' book. What could people say? They said: 'May they not have died in vain'; 'No more war'; a simple '*Merci*'. An English school party had been here. A teacher noted how impressed the school had been. But the pupils seemed at a loss. Nothing in their lives, not even the televised coffins arriving from Afghanistan, bore any relation to this. I read their comments: 'A lot of them'; 'Sorry . . . really'; 'Love all round'; 'Wow! Many bricks and dead people.'

# 13. HONOUR

I still knew almost nothing about Edmund Ashworth. The family story was that he'd been made up to Lance-Corporal because he'd been a good steady bowler on the local cricket team, and so he'd be good at throwing grenades. It was also said that he died because another soldier was ill and Edmund offered to take his place in the front line.

From the book stacks of the London Library in St James's Square I dug out the official war history of the Duke of Wellington's regiment during the First World War. It was published in Halifax in 1920, with the regimental badge on the front. The badge had an elephant in the middle, labelled Hindoostan. The frontispiece was a pair of photographs of Ypres Cloth Hall: as it was in 1914 and in 1918, all but destroyed.

The regiment meant nothing to me. I sometimes went past the barracks on a Saturday afternoon, on my way to watch Rugby League matches. In a passing fashion for motorbike racing, Halifax had a speedway team. It was called The Dukes, after the regiment. Their track was at the Halifax Town soccer club's ground. I sold crisps and ice cream there as the loudspeakers played 'Twelfth Street Rag'. The vague connection didn't influence me when I was called up to do National Service. I was determined not to go into any infantry regiment if I could help it, and especially not the Duke of Wellington's. In those days, I was busy trying to detach myself from Yorkshire.

In August 1914, 650 men reported for duty at Halifax schools. The battalion Edmund joined were Territorials. The Territorial Army was founded in 1908 as fears about Germany mounted. At 1.30 pm, on 5 August, Edmund's battalion marched down the steep granite setts to Halifax railway station, to go to their designated port of Hull. 'There was no public send-off,' Captain P.G. Bales, the war historian, writes. After all the scares, 'the war had come so suddenly that people hardly seemed to realise what was happening'.

Kitchener, the newly appointed secretary of state for war, was suspicious of the Territorials as 'weekend soldiers'. So Edmund and his colleagues spent their time at Hull doing odd jobs, digging trenches, guarding the docks, trying to round up supposed German spies.

Only in April 1915 did the battalion leave the north of England. By the summer they were in the Ypres salient, the only corner of Belgium not conquered by the Germans. To abandon the town of Ypres would have straightened out the line and cut down cross-fire in the salient. But it became a point of principle for the British that Ypres should not be taken. And it never was, though in the Third Battle of Ypres, better known as Passchendaele, about 200,000 British soldiers died in the mud in late 1917, trying to break the German line. The German defenders lost almost as many. Sometimes Hitler was in the German trenches.

A map in Bales's book shows the lines the battalion occupied. The soldiers gave them names from home: Barnsley Road, Colne Valley, Skipton Road, Huddersfield Road. There was little other comfort. The battalion arrived, Bales reports, keen to 'bag a Bosch'. They only had two old Maxim machine guns, so they mostly relied on rifles. Hand grenades were 'just coming to the fore' – and, with them, Edmund Ashworth's old skills as a bowler. The Germans had mortars and the battalion 'had nothing effective to retaliate with'. From war to war, British politicians have consistently asked men to fight without proper armaments.

In the salient, water lay close to the surface. No orders had been given to put in drainage. Sometimes the gap between the opposing lines was only about 60 yards. Grenades were hurled across it. On 26 August 1915, a message was thrown back: 'Dear Tommy – Brest-Litovsk fallen today. Rippelin, Lieut.' That same day, the battalion moved back for a rest period. 'The cleaning of buttons was instituted for the first time since the battalion left England.' Then it was back to the front line.

At the end of October, the rains began. The trenches were barely above the level of the canal. Water poured in. Earthworks collapsed. The wounded had to lie in the mud until they could be picked up after dark, assuming they were still alive. The Germans pumped water out of their own trenches and into the battalion's. No one had planned for this. Men stuck in mud had to be pulled free, leaving their boots behind. They then had to fight in their socks. Soldiers were supposed to put protective grease on their feet, but there was nowhere dry to do this. All there was plenty of was rum. In such conditions, the Duke of Wellington's held the line in November and December 1915.

'A man had a ghastly prospect in front of him,' Bales writes, 'when his turn came to form part of a front-line garrison for forty-eight hours. For all that time he would be thoroughly soaked and terribly cold; his boots would be full of water, he would stand in water and mud; physical pain, mental weariness and bodily fatigue would be his constant burden. The chances were that he would not complete his tour of duty – that before that time was up he would succumb to the snipers, or be on his way to hospital, a physical wreck.' One officer took twenty-four men forward for their two-day stint. He came back with four. 'In that hell,' Bales reports, the soldiers of the battalion – very Yorkshire – were 'quiet, tight-lipped and dogged', with occasional dry jokes. They just 'held on'.

Somewhere in all this Lance-Corporal Ashworth was killed. Six days after he died, the German army attacked with poison gas and artillery. Next year the battalion went south to the Somme and fought at Thiepval. Here, 101 were killed, 463 wounded; 155 are included on the Lutyens monument's scroll of the missing. The battalion came back to the Ypres salient for the renewed miseries of Passchendaele.

Captain Bales's book is dedicated to 'all ranks' in the battalion who died. But class and rank prevailed even in death. In the appendices, officers who died are listed with all the details of their service. Warrant officers get briefer details. Anyone below the rank of company quartermaster-sergeant is lumped into the 'summary of casualties'. Between 8 July and 20 December, the figures are: of officers, seven killed, seven wounded; of other ranks, 116 killed, 206 wounded, four missing. Honours are listed differently, by the ranking of the award. Private A. Poulter's Victoria Cross heads the list. Many of the names of the men who were honoured are the surnames I grew up among: Sykes, Parkinson, Bailey, Binns, Metcalfe, Mitchell, Dobson, Gledhill, Hartley, Jessop, Greaves, Shackleton. There are two Barkers.

In the newspaper files of the British Library, in north London, I tried to glean more from the 1914 and 1915 editions of the *Hebden Bridge Times*. The classifieds were full of the names of firms I half-remember. 'Matthew Sheard, coal merchants' still supply Hebden with its coal, not now for textile mills but for household stoves and fires. The film programme of the Royal Electric Theatre – a hut my parents called 'the fleapit' – included *Orders Under Seal*. The newspaper's leader on the outbreak of war – written, I assume, by Edmund and Will's father, Handley Ashworth – was headed 'Teutonic Ambition: Aiming at Britain'. He wrote that the war 'is not a question of Servia, nor of Russia. It is a question of isolating England in order that when isolated she may be compelled to submit to German dictation.'

In an item on the government order for Territorials to report for duty, Alfred Dehner, from a Hebden Bridge Anglo-German family, was listed as one of those who, in August 1914, had already done so. Edmund Ashworth and six other teachers enrolled in September. Also in September, anti-German riots broke out in Keighley, over the hill from Pecket. The rioters attacked pork butchers (both German and English), pawnbrokers, jewellers and a bank. The mayor said he saw 'no excuse for English people to attack in a cowardly and un-English way the houses of unfortunate Germans who happened to be in England'. The first in a series of weekly newsletters appeared in the *Hebden Bridge Times* 'from a local Territorial' – who must be Edmund, reporting cheerfully on life near Grimsby, where he is sleeping in a chapel and having 'quite a jolly time of it with ragtime songs on the organ'.

Slowly the deaths began to rise. Private J.W. Greenwood was the first. He 'fell asleep' during 'the Kaiser's vicious attack'. The paper's back pages started to carry more and more photographs of the dead – 'the fallen heroes' – usually in the Sunday best they wore in the studio before they left. Some letters escaped censorship and told of nightmarish events: 'The first 20 minutes were such as I never had before, and hope never to have again.' The front pages were full of report on flower shows, the triumphs of the Hebden Bridge brass band and the proceedings of the town gas committee. In the back pages, the deaths now filled column after column. Of the three sons in one widow's 'patriotic household', one was dead, one missing, one wounded.

In early December, now under the *nom de plume* 'Hebden', Edmund was still writing columns for the paper. He tried to put a good face on things.

His party, back from the front line, 'were welcomed by a cheerful blaze' in the hut they went to recuperate in. 'On the whole it proved to be a pleasant eight days, in spite of the quagmire we had to wade through whenever we planted our feet out of doors, and the inevitable coating of mud on the wooden floor, and the rain that trickled through the ceiling just where the howling wind ripped away the protective tarpaulin.' But he also criticised the wasteful way rations were distributed and blamed the contractors who supplied them. He says that 'a pal remarked to me, "there'll be a h___ of a lot to answer for *après la guerre*".' He ended by saying this might be his last report before Christmas, and said he was sure that 'the Tommies out here . . . will join me in wishing merry Christmas to the people at home'. He didn't live to see that Christmas.

In the issue of 25 December 1915, days after Edmund's death, I read that the *Messiah* is to be sung at one of the Methodist chapels. At the workhouse, it is reported, the inmates sing 'God bless our boys in khaki/God bless our boys in blue.' On the back page is Edmund Ashworth, in a reproduction of the photograph we brought back from Hebden Bridge after Sally's mother died. There were more tributes than I'd seen in any other local death notice. Lance-Corporal Ashworth was strong, cheerful and witty, so a fellow-soldier ('WHM') writes; he was 'in a class by himself'. His cricketing days were recalled with pride. His lieutenant wrote to say that Edmund was his right-hand man. For grenades, he 'won the individual throwing test' and was 'streets ahead of any of us'. Edmund had just returned to the front after a grenade accident.

His papers had just gone in for a commission, and had been approved, when he was killed. In an obituary, his father took comfort in the thought that 'Now he has accepted a higher Commission. His death was such as he would have wished for, if it should be his lot to go.' W.H.M. wrote that 'He met his death with the calm indifference he always showed. At 6.30 am on the morning of December 13th, he had just finished giving the rations out to his section and was stretching his weary and wet limbs when the bullet of a German sniper pierced his heart. He said, "I am hit; fetch the stretcher bearers," and then peacefully passed to rest.' On 14 December, a party of soldiers took his body to 'our ever-increasing cemetery'.

'His remains lay just a little west of the Yser Canal, among many more of our gallant comrades.'

# 14. OBELISK

Stoodley Pike is a memorial to peace, not war. It was built on its bleak hilltop to celebrate Napoleon's defeat, in 1814, at the Leipzig 'Battle of the Nations', and his subsequent exile to the island of Elba. In the upper Calder valley, the good news was that the wartime blockade of ports was over. British goods could again be sold into the continent, most notably wool and cotton fabrics. Of course, Leipzig turned out to be not quite the end of the story. The builders suspended their work on the Pike in March 1815, when Napoleon escaped from Elba. But after his Hundred Days' triumph, Napoleon met his Waterloo. Work on the Pike resumed. It was completed later that year.

There had been some kind of cairn or pillar on the site before. Some say it commemorated the brief Peace of Amiens, signed in 1802. During this pause in the post-revolutionary conflict, the Westminster parliament repealed income tax, which had been introduced to raise money for the French wars. It also passed the Health and Morals of Apprentices Act. This forbade cotton mills (like those in Cragg Vale) from hiring pauper children under the age of nine; their working day was limited to twelve hours, and they were not allowed to work at night.

The Amiens treaty didn't last. The French 'Army of England' was mustered, and an invasion fleet was brought together at Boulogne, ready to invade. Britain re-introduced income tax. Napoleon crowned himself emperor. By 1806, Britain and France were blockading each other's ports. British textile mills began to shut down: the blockades squeezed the inflow of American raw cotton.

The 1814 Pike was built by public subscription. All the old names were on the list: Sutcliffe, Ingham, Greenwood, Uttley and the rest, including a Gibson of Gibson mill. The foundation stone was laid with full Masonic honours. But this first Pike was a fairly modest construction. It was struck by lightning in 1854 and fell down. It was rebuilt as the tall, dark obelisk you now see. The builder, this time around, was Lewis Crabtree of Hebden Bridge.

The money for the new Pike came mostly from the cotton men of Todmorden, especially John Fielden, one of the largest cotton manufacturers in Britain. The inscription carved into the Pike was apparently drafted by Fielden himself. The obelisk is described as a 'Peace Monument'. It is noted that 'By a strange coincidence the Pike fell on the day the Russian Ambassador left London before the declaration of war with Russia in 1854 [the Crimean war], and it was rebuilt when peace was proclaimed in 1856.'

John Fielden was the very model of a beneficent manufacturer, helping to push the Ten Hours Act through parliament. To the Fielden family, Todmorden also owes its stupendous town hall, a cathedral-sized Unitarian church (where Mrs Gaskell's minister-husband used to preach) and the bizarre Dobroyd Castle. When trade was bad, Fielden built a road up towards the Pike – you can still spot the traces of it. The road was responding to no real demand from local transport. But it gave some kind of work.

Fielden was a Liberal in his politics. Under the local laws of popular scepticism, this meant that his workforce were mostly Tory (not that many of them had the vote). The Fieldens' former Waterside factory – where young John himself started working for his father at the age of nine – was once a place of pilgrimage for those who wanted to see a cotton mill. That new-fangled business. Now the liveliest business in the neighbourhood is a Morrison's superstore.

The Fieldens' obelisk is 120 feet high, and it rises 1,307 feet above sea level. It is the Fielden hallmark, stamped on the Pennine horizon. You are hardly ever in a location where you can't see it. The reason why it's there is, by now, a complete mystery to almost everyone you speak to in Hebden or Todmorden. In my schooldays, I had no idea, either.

It is years since I walked up to it. I begin near Hebden Bridge's beautifully preserved railway station, and go along past the building that used to house the grim Co-op abattoir. I am surrounded by a miscellaneous assortment of 1920s and 1930s semi-detached houses, added to by 1990s infill. This is not a part of the Hebden you see on postcards, though the cards often show the view *from* here to the top-and-bottom houses on the hillside across the valley. The camera may not always lie, but it knows how to massage the truth.

I'm not sure I've got the right path through scrubby fields and patchy wood. I come to a television booster mast. This was built to permit the people in the valley bottom to get BBC2 and Channel 4, which were otherwise blocked by the Pennines. I know now that I'm on the right road. If I took the track down, I'd be at Weasel Hall. Behind me is the hamlet where William Barker built a dye works and launched Hebden's ready-made clothing trade. I turn up towards the Erringden hillside. Erringden is a vast, barely inhabited hill parish. Centuries ago, when Hebden Bridge scarcely existed, Erringden was a feudal deer park. The approach to the abattoir is called Palace House Road. The name comes from a reworking of the original 'Palisser's House'. The meaning was long forgotten. It designated the house of the man who looked after the palisade around the deer park.

The outlook gets ever more magnificent as you go upwards along the hillside. The wide fields of Erringden are marked out by black, weathered dry-stone walls. Here and there, wind-battered copses help keep out the wind. The sky is all grey with cloud. As I walk into the wind, it blows steadily, but today at least it is warm. At long intervals, stone farm houses, many of them seventeenth-century, stretch out towards the looming Pike.

Erringden Grange is one of the largest. It is a small hamlet in its own right. The farmhouse itself is in good shape, but the barn and the enclave of farm-workers' cottages look half-abandoned. I have vague memories of a family connection. Before he lived at Weasel Hall, Ira Greenwood lived at Grange. As I walk, I think back to family tales. The story, for example, of the man who took so long a-wooing a young woman – visiting her every Sunday, at her home, for years – that he came down the lane one day to see her, and saw a large crowd gathered at the house. 'What's all this about, then?' 'Nay, lad, tha's tekken too long about it. She's getting wed.'

Or the story of another young woman, who was jilted on her wedding day. The family went on to Halifax, regardless, to eat the wedding breakfast. After all, they'd paid for it. They also shared out the presents. The man who abandoned his intended bride was immediately fired from his job. I don't know what happened to him afterwards, but she apparently never married and died early. Her funeral was held on a bitterly cold, winter's day. The coffin had to be taken by sledge. In the cemetery, the ground was frozen solid. It was a struggle to lower the coffin and cover it. 'Nay, lass,' my grandfather Barker said, 'it were a right trouble trying to get thee wed. Now it's just as much trouble getting thee buried.'

Further along, at the Mittens farm, a surprising array of trees, bushes and flowers has been planted all around, to turn the farm into a house. The farm names are a folk-poem: Grange, Pinnacle, Kershaw, Swillington, Lower Rough Head, Rake Head (which used to be the parish workhouse). Along the sides of the track, the stone walls are falling down. Sheep are penned into their fields by plain or barbed wire. A walker coming towards me, with a pair of walking sticks, stares at me glumly when I say hello. He seems not to know the rule that you always say hello back – or, once upon a time, 'nah then'.

As I go higher, I can see far across the hills to Heptonstall church and Cock Hill, the last hill before the road from Hebden dips down towards Haworth and Keighley. Snippets of sunshine interleave the grey clouds. You can tell how big Stoodley Pike is – only 30 feet lower than Thiepval – by the way its height scarcely seems to change as you get nearer to it. I'm out of the fields now. I pass the remains of Johnny Gap, farm, which was the site of a local stock fair, and cross the old Deer Leap, another marker from the deer park centuries.

I'm now on to the open moor. Shreds of wool are caught on the grey rocks. Towards the Pike, the wind stiffens. I am on the edge of Lancashire. I see a clutch of walkers coming up from that side of the ridge. They end up as a row of little black figures on the skyline beside the Pike. I think the Yorkshire walk has been easier. A lark rises, sings, then plunges back into the coarse moor grass. A buzzard flaps across. It has hardly rained for weeks – which is unusual hereabouts – so the path, often boggy, is good to walk on.

Whenever I've visited it, I have always found the Pike a very gloomy edifice, seen near to. A balcony runs round it, 40 feet up. If you want to reach this, you go up an unlovely, unlit newel stair. I decide to give this a miss today. So do the other walkers who've now reached the Pike. Even to walk round the base is a struggle against the stiff gusts of wind. Football graffiti have been sprayed on all four sides: 'Man City.' Most of the walkers are going back into Lancashire. They say they hope for cups of tea, once they're down. The only other walker going the other way says he looks forward to 'a good bag of chips' in Hebden Bridge.

I cut down the hillside to where I know I can pick up a bus. It is awkward, tussocky walking, until I reach a better road at Lower Rough Head. This is still a serious farm. In the yard I see three huge tractors, two 4×4s, a quad bike and a truck. In a lower field there are a couple of perky new calves. From here the road drops steeply down and into hillside woodland. Below me I see the main Hebden–Todmorden road and the glint of the Rochdale canal.

I decide to go back along the canal. I find myself transported into the Hebden of the hippie pioneer days. On a neglected, ill-defined terrain between the canal and the demolished Callis mill, a little colony survives.

A new housing estate is due to be built where the mill was. But a sign at the canal edge says 'Callis Community'. A high tepee has the remains of a fire outside it, with chopped logs arranged as a circle of seats around this. Little triangular flags flutter from a frame outside the tepee, on which a gauzy red dress is hanging to dry. On a pub-type trestle table, half painted pink, is a large serving spoon and the rest of the paint in a tin. A shovel leans against the table. Four kayaks are tied up to the towpath. Two red lifebelts have been hung on a small birch-tree. Three bikes, not chained up, lie next to them. Three wheelbarrows stand in a row. In an old shed there are yet more bikes, including children's models. Other sheds store wood. Dog roses mark off the community from the towpath. Another sign says 'Permaculture Plants Sale Now'.

In the background is the constant hum of traffic along the main road. On the track to the road an old boat has been abandoned. There are also a battered old white van and a Mitsubishi 4×4. At the moment, the community is deserted. The inhabitants are out at work or collecting children at school, I'm told.

I walk along towards Hebden Bridge. I pass several dozen permanently parked narrowboats. Some are decorated prettily. Others are very
plain and look almost seaworthy. A few are for sale: asking price between
£18,000 and £28,000. Like the tepee hamlet, the narrowboats are almost
deserted right now. Most of the boat people have put plant pots on the
cabin roofs. Many of them are cyclists: either their bikes are here, or the
frames to hold them.

I go past Hebble End mill, once a textile firm, now the headquarters
of a company that supplies builders and local councils with items made
from recycled plastic: gutters, drainpipes, park seats. In the upper room
of the Nelson pub, across the street, I went to scout meetings for a couple
of years. The pub is now closed and converted into houses. The next mill
I come to, a few yards further along the canal bank, is home to several
eccentric or ecological enterprises.

I am due to meet Polly Webber here. She runs the Alternative
Technology Centre. Many people have told me that Polly represents all
that's best about the new Hebden. I'm early for the meeting, so I wander
down to look at the other businesses within the same mill building. The
(locked) shop of www.wiccanbroomcupboard.com offers 'custom-made
staffs, wands and swords'. The window display is of six varied witches'
brooms. A placard says: 'If the door is open then I'm here/ Shout my
name and I will appear/ Be Blessed Tony.' With its belts and quivers,
the Tan My Hide shop smells of fine leather. You can buy a packet of
Heritage Wild Flowers, a hedgehog house, a robin nester, a 15-litre box
of Ecover washing-up liquid, a fuel cell science kit or a toy wind-vane.
A noticeboard advertises: 'Landscape artist available to do commissions.
Have a painting of your house'; 'Nora the Gentle Builder'; 'Join a local
Eco-Team'. I feel sure that Willow Woman, from John Morrison's *View
from the Bridge*, would have shopped here.

Polly's daughter, Abby, tall and rangy, is sitting on a seat outside
the Alternative Technology Centre. We talk about what it means to be
local. She says, 'I'm from all over. I've been here twenty-five years, but
you're only local after the first person you met dies.' Polly comes out to
join us. She is charmingly unaggressive, unlike many eco-campaigners.
She holds to the definition that you're only local 'if you have Sutcliffes or
Greenwoods in your family tree'.

Polly has run the Hebden Bridge centre for more than a decade. The core of her work, she says, is not propaganda but information. In schools, she leads workshops about renewable energy. 'We have a very good schools website.' When she first came to Hebden Bridge, she helped to set up the Circus Factory business in the vacant Mitchell mill, making juggling bags and clubs. She got fed up with that. She 'never wanted to be seen as a hippie. To bring about change, you mustn't just spread doom and gloom. You must create a place like this where ordinary people will come in and not simply walk off. I don't want to preach to the converted.'

Polly grew up in Rochdale, though she knew people in Hebden. She went down to Devon for fifteen years. 'One son is still down there.' Her husband wanted to come north again. 'But I said I wouldn't do it without proper housing and central heating.'

She is attractively realistic. She recognises the divisions *within* the newcomers. It can be difficult, she says, 'especially when you're dealing with people who think they've got right on their side'. And then there are the newcomer/local divisions. 'Every presentation, every study, has brought up the divided community.' She thinks there are now three main divisions: the locals, the older-style newcomers and the new professionals. The latter two groups are at odds, for example, over the scheme to put allotments on open land that faces a row of well-to-do houses.

Polly used to be a neighbour of Chris Ratcliffe's on Windsor Road, and helped with the campaign to protect the local open space from developers. She decided she would prefer to be able to get away from all that. She now lives on the hillside that leads up to Blackshaw Head. I think she doesn't like to be slotted into any one category. 'We want to talk to people about their electricity bills. We want farmers to come and talk to us.'

Abby picks up her mother's point about the social and ethical divisions. 'People come to Hebden, and then go – because the place is so opinionated. And about being local or not: there's no problem face to face, but then, behind your back or when you leave the room. . . .' She leaves the rest unsaid. 'Many people come for the schools. Some Asian couples come to Hebden, but they soon leave.'

# 15. TEARS

St George's Square, now thought of as the middle of Hebden Bridge, is the triangular site of an old mill, pulled down years ago. The existing Bridge mill is still at one end. At the other end, the old White Horse pub was also pulled down, as part of the local council's then-policy of demolition. A new road would have been driven through. Hebden lost a pub, as it's turned out, but gained a car park. (Most Hebden conversations contain at least one paragraph about parking.) The White Horse used to be the handiest place to go to during breaks in any dances they held in the Co-op Hall, on the top floor of the big headquarters building the Hebden Bridge Co-op erected between 1876 and 1889.

The Co-op's collapse, in 1967, was the low point in Hebden's recent history. Until then, it supplied most people with most things. It was brought down largely by the Co-ops' inbuilt, almost inbred, inertia in competing with new firms and new trends. But the death blow was the discovery that the managing secretary, Frederick Chatburn – a pillar of old Hebden – had for years been treating local people's savings accounts as his own. It's always been a mystery – to me, at least – what he spent the money on. Some say rent-boys in York. In May 1967, at Leeds Crown Court, he was sentenced to four years' imprisonment.

A few months later, the members of the Co-op voted to wind the society up. All the staff were dismissed. In April 1968, all the buildings of all the branches went for auction. The outlying branches were usually just a shop and a storeroom. They went for derisory prices, sometimes as low as £130. All, I think, are now houses. The three-storey central block, with its handsome clock, was withdrawn from sale when no one would offer more than £8,500. The block was sold privately, later. Other shops moved into the ground floor. The upper floors became a four-star hotel for a while. Now they are flats. It's claimed that eventually all the Co-op savers, or their heirs, got their money back. But it was the end of the old 'Co-op and chapel culture'.

In the centre of St George's Square a huge version of a fustian cutter's knife has been erected. The knife is tilted at the correct angle to work as the gnomon of a sundial, with the hours marked out on the pavement. At least, that's the way it works when the Hebden sun is strong enough – which isn't all that often. As with everything in Hebden, the creation of this tribute to the textile-worker past became a big issue: pro or anti.

Today, as I go into the square, I see little platoons of serious walkers, setting off with their staves. The cafés on the square have put out their tables: optimistic, even in July. The fustian knife has become a focus of a kind that neither the advocates nor the opponents expected: a tribute to 'Sharky' from her friends. Some pink and green balloons have been tied to the knife. Flowers lie there, drooping. There are numerous tea-lights all around, and all of them are out. The scene looks like a more forceful version of the tributes you now see at the point on the roadside where someone has been killed in a car or bike accident.

This isn't quite what has happened. The *Hebden Bridge Times* front-page splash was 'Sister Dies in Balcony Fall'. Sarah Royle's family moved to Hebden from Manchester twenty years before. Both parents were now dead, leaving the three sisters, Sarah, Johanna and Premsa, who all went to Calder High School. Sarah, the eldest – nickname Sharky – had gone out to Australia to work. In a hotel in Singapore, she was celebrating an England victory in an early round of soccer's 2010 World Cup when she fell off a balcony. Joanna and Premsa raised enough money to go out and see her, but Sarah died from her injuries. Why she fell still remained unclear. The insurance company wouldn't guarantee the costs of either the hospital or a flight back for Sarah's body. Joanna and Premsa came back on their own. Friends and family began trying to raise more money.

The sheets of paper tied to the knife are damp with dew. 'Sharky!!! I will meet you up there for a bloody good strop!! All my love from

Emily xxxxxxx', 'Goodbye my sweet Sarah – Pam' and a poem entitled 'Beeswing':

> She was that rare thing
> Fine as a beeswing
> So fine a breath of wind might blow her away
> She was a free child
> Running wild
> She said 'As long as there's no price on love I'll stay
> And you wouldn't want it any other way' . . .

The next time I go into the square, a week later, it is full of members of the Sealed Knot, getting ready to re-enact the 'Battle of Heptonstall' between Roundheads and Cavaliers. They are busy trying to get their gear ready for the uphill climb. Growing up in Hebden, we were always told that the ruins of Heptonstall old church were the relics of a cannon attack by Cromwell's men. In fact, they were what was left after a nineteenth-century bishop decided that swelling congregations and storm damage demanded a new church. This was duly built alongside. I never remember hearing anything at all about a 'battle'. Maybe a skirmish? But clearly it is a nice day's outing for several dozen stout men.

The Sharky tributes have gone. I speak to a steward, who doesn't know why. A by-passer, overhearing us, says how 'mawkish' he thinks the tributes were. It made no difference to the re-enactors whether the stuff was there or not. It emerges, a few days later, that the removal is due to some officious, tidy-minded man from Calderdale council. The council apologises. The Royles manage to raise the money, all the same. 'Community' is the only way to describe what happened. Sharky's body came back to the place where she'd grown up. As the weeks passed, the fustian knife in St George's Square became *the* place for youthful grievers over other deaths to lay flowers.

'Community' is a word often spoken in Hebden. In 2010, a documentary film about Hebden called *Shed Your Tears and Walk Away* made people pause. The film was first shown in March that year at the Picture House in Hebden Bridge, with re-showings afterwards. Some anxious public question-times followed, often about 'community'. The film was reviewed in the national press, though it had hardly any national screening.

The *Daily Telegraph*'s reviewer called it 'one of the saddest films I've seen in a very long time'. The *Daily Mirror* took it as evidence that 'Aside from being a haven for achingly trendy bohemians, the Yorkshire village of Hebden Bridge is becoming known for something else – its serious drink and drugs problem.' *The Times* called the film 'a confessional for damaged souls'. The *Guardian* called it 'passionate and sometimes despairing'. The film, by documentary maker Jez Lewis, was an abrupt antidote to all the publicity articles which said, almost interminably, that Hebden Bridge was the fourth-funkiest place on the planet (British Airways' in-flight magazine), the lesbian capital of Britain (the *Guardian*'s Saturday magazine) or Great Town of the Year (the Academy of Urbanism).

Jez Lewis is a refugee from the first stage of Hebden's post-industrial transformation. He moved to Hebden in 1972, aged five, with his mother. She was trying to escape from what he calls 'a bad marriage' in Cirencester, in the Cotswolds. She changed her name from 'Hodge' and arrived in Hebden with five children and a suitcase. She'd answered a small ad for lodgers, placed by one of the first of the new wave of outsiders, who lived on the moor edge at a row of cottages called Foster Clough.

The father hired a private detective and traced her, in spite of the name change. The upshot was a divorce and a painful custody battle. The oldest child, a daughter, stayed with the father; the other four (including young Jez) stayed with the mother. Later the family moved down into Hebden Bridge itself, to a street which was called Industrial Street when the Co-op built it, but which was called Garden Terrace after it was renovated. Jez went to school locally but, for him, Hebden left bad memories of families without fathers, the uncertain boundaries of hippie family life, and all-too-accessible drugs.

He left the place after his schooldays, with 'no intention of going back'. He studied at the universities of East London and Sussex. He did research work for various public bodies, including the Blair government's Social Exclusion Unit. He went on to work with the highly regarded documentary-maker Nick Broomfield. Jez helped to write and produce Broomfield's moving documentary *Ghosts*, about the Chinese cockle-pickers who were drowned in Morecambe Bay in early 2004 when the tide swept in.

After growing up in Hebden, among 'the poorest of the poor', Jez didn't buy into the local publicists' Panglossian line that all is for the best in the best of all possible worlds. He thinks of Hebden Bridge, for many people, as a place marked by a 'narrowness of outlook and physical opportunity'. To judge by what he was hearing from Hebden, there was much addiction to drink or drugs among young people. Many he knew died young. His mother had by now moved back to South Wales, where she grew up. From time to time, she would phone Jez, who was now living in Suffolk with his partner and two children, to let him know that another of his schooldays friends had died. After yet another phone call, he decided to try to make a documentary.

At first he saw it as a 15-minute TV short, but the idea grew. BBC1 and BBC2 and Channel 4 all gave his documentary pitch the thumbs down. He felt so committed that he put up his home a collateral for a loan in order to make it. It cost £70,000; he put up 51 per cent; the rest of the money came from East Anglia Arts. By now he was forty.

Emma is the young woman whose fate who prompted the film. She is a childhood friend who died of a heroin overdose. Jez remembers her as a very bright girl. It may be that the overdose was accidental, but she had attempted suicide twice in the past. Jez thought back to other deaths, over the years. His one-time next-door neighbour, Peter, stepped in front of a bus. Another neighbour, Mark, jumped in front of a train. Bill, one of Jez's closest friends from Hebden, hanged himself. So did Nicky, who lived two doors down from Emma. 'That was just on our street,' Jez says. A little further off, 'Tez purposely overdosed, Swinny overdosed though presumably by accident, Kurt hanged himself, Gina committed suicide, several people I didn't know have been found hanging in the woods, and it is still going on after twenty years.'

Jez says he has 'a deeply ambivalent view' of Hebden. He maintains he has 'great affection' for it. But 'it is a place I arrived at as my home life fell apart, and where too many of my friends have perished'. He made his 90-minute film over the course of a year. When he started making trips back to Hebden, he was shocked by the state of things. 'The situation is worse than ever; worse than I could have imagined.' His conclusion: 'What twenty years ago was a handful of ne'er-do-well youths, drinking cider and smoking dope, has become a nightmare of hard drink, harder drugs and random deaths, affecting all generations.'

He sees himself as growing up with 'a foot in each camp' in Hebden – the hippyish arrivals and the local working class. 'This enables me to see the process of colonisation of the time from both sides.' He is hardest on Hebden's hippie inheritance. In a background note to the film, he writes:

Perhaps that quirky and tolerant legacy of the 1970s hippies is actually the root of the problem. They came from all over the country, indeed the world; some to live in small semi-communes, others more interested in lifestyles with no rules. A liberalism developed which countenanced not just freedom of choice and free love, but hard drugs and sexual licentiousness. Hebden Bridge became infected with a squalid kind of hedonism, a playground for people who refused to grow up. And those people have raised a generation who never learned how to grow up.

The effects have rippled out and diffused into the local working class population, while disillusionment at meagre prospects and tough home lives combines with feelings of physical isolation, claustrophobia and boredom. Jobs are few and poorly paid, divorce and separation rates are high, and house prices have done a U-turn, now leaving locals behind as wealthier people move into the town and take control.

No hot-gospel Methodist preacher could have put it better. Almost everyone in the film seems, most of the time, to have a can of Carlsberg Special Brew to hand. They are usually photographed hanging around the town centre park. No one is preaching old-time temperance to them. They live on benefits, odd jobs and petty theft. They are good at logic-chopping. One says he only steals from supermarkets, never from small shops, almost as if he's doing his bit to fight capitalism. The courts tend not to agree.

Sally and I catch up with the film at a showing in London, at the Institute of Contemporary Arts, in The Mall. This is an odd place to see it, especially as the ICA reception desk don't even seem to know it is on. (The ICA is undergoing one of its periodic internal upheavals.) But we finally make it. A similar film could probably have been made about some parts of London. But metropolitan guilt only spreads so far, it seems: only ten of us are at that evening's showing. So far as we can tell, we are the only two with any northern connection.

The showing opens with a Yorkshire tourism advertisement. Clichés are not easily shifted. And *Shed Your Tears and Walk Away* does begin with a beautiful aerial shot of Hebden Bridge, nestling among its hills. But this is the film maker's irony. There is no more light amid the gloom.

Jez's is the only voice in the film apart from the men and women he's observing. He doesn't interview local spokespersons: doctors, councillors, social workers, therapists, church workers. He is presenting the story of this group of about a dozen people, mostly men, who spend much of their day doing nothing but drink beer and smoke 'skunk' (marijuana). The film's title is a quote from a remark made by one of the two core interviewees: Michael Silcock, nicknamed 'Silly'. The other main figure is 'Cass'. Both are now in their forties. They have tried, and failed, to get off the drink and the drugs. Hardly anyone else in the group seems to be even trying. They are just killing time – and, in the not very long run, themselves.

The film is a case study of almost unmitigated despair, except that, towards the end, it seems that Cass may be pulling out of the deep dark hole he has got himself into. The film claims that Hebden Bridge is particularly prone to suicide.

This claim is hard to pin down. So far as I can make out, West Yorkshire has slightly worse suicide rates than the national figure; within West Yorkshire, the entire borough of Calderdale, including Halifax, is slightly worse than that; and the upper Calder valley (not just Hebden Bridge) is slightly worse again. The statistical differences are tiny. They certainly did not justify the headline on an *Independent* feature article: 'Why Has Hebden Bridge Become Suicide Central?'

There's little doubt that suicide can be almost like an infectious disease, among some groups. I think that this is Jez Lewis's own interpretation of what he has portrayed in Hebden.

The film is hard to watch. We quickly come to the flowers at Sam Jones's funeral. Sam collapsed and died in the street while the film was being made. He had been drinking and taking drugs. He was twenty-five. Sam's brother Liam remembers the way Sam was. This is a double dose of melancholy because we, the viewers, know that Liam also died after the film was complete. His mother Michelle grew up in Hebden, on the same hilltop council estate as Lesley Jones and Christine Jackson. She has four other children. She is quoted as saying: 'Sam used to drink a lot and take cocaine, but he had stopped for about ten weeks. He'd had a row with his girlfriend, and I think he thought he could drink and take the same amounts he did before. I carry a lot of guilt because I was so wrapped up in my other son, Liam, who was a heroin addict at the time, that I didn't notice Sam's problem. If I'd known how it was going to turn out here, I'd have got my children and run.'

In the film Michelle appears to treat Liam, at the age of twenty-seven, like an errant child. She herself says she feels excluded by the social changes in Hebden. 'Even at the playground, the outsiders have taken over. They stand there like a little click. They took over the parents' association.' It's a blame game.

Jez says that many young people in Hebden drink a bottle of vodka a day. On film, Liam says: 'I may be fucking drinking, but I'm not drinking all the time. And I'm not injecting ever again.' His mother's take on things is slightly different: she seems pleased that he is now only using clean needles. One of Michelle's daughters, a baby-faced sixteen, is filmed listening to Liam as he tells his tale of woe. She says: 'The trouble is he has never grown up. He behaves like a fifteen-year-old.' Listening and watching the film, it's hard to differ from her diagnosis.

Sam's is not the only funeral. We see Nicola Keetin, happy, bright and pretty. The next thing we know is that she has been burnt to death in her boyfriend's flat. Yet more flowers.

# 16. HEPTONSTALL

I find Michael Silcock ('Silly') the most intriguing of the group Jez Lewis portrays. The others are often much younger. You wonder why they don't simply leave Hebden, if life is so tedious there, and get a job. After all, this is what huge numbers of young people did, over the years. That is why Hebden's population had fallen so steadily.

The answer seems to be that they are 'scared'. It is hard to know what they are scared of. Drinking their Special Brew on the park, they may have felt they had some sort of outsiderish standing: half-baked beats or punks. In fact, the rest of the population walks on by, and sheds no tears at all. I don't know how many deal in drugs as well as consuming them. Probably most of them, part of the time.

'Silly' — so called from his surname, not from his behaviour — seems to me the most self-aware of the group. He had come to Hebden, but he wasn't born here. His life includes a stint in the French Foreign Legion. In Jez Lewis's film, his awareness of his predicament doesn't help. It seems to make him the group's most despairing member. I decide to try to see him.

By now it is well over a year since Jez Lewis filmed him. In one of the closing scenes, Silly's intended marriage is broken off at the very last minute because he is drinking so much. His fiancée opens a can of beer to drown her sorrow.

I am surprised to find where Silly lives now. It is a very new, attractively built block of housing association flats at the edge of Heptonstall. I am a bit early, so I walk round the village first. As always, I try to find the coiner David Hartley's grave, among the flat black memorial stones. This means pacing out the distance from the porch of the ruined medieval church. But I find it.

I decide to look for Sylvia Plath's grave, also. I haven't visited it for many years. I go round the back of the Victorian church, face on into the rain that the wind is blowing across the hills. Here is the newer graveyard. There is no special indication of where the Plath grave is. I have to ask for guidance from David Griffiths, a young man at a nearby house. As we walk between the rows of graves, he tells me he is from Somerset but he came to live in Heptonstall five years ago. His partner is from Oldham and wanted to come back to her 'home territory'. David works as a male nurse. He commutes to Ashton-under-Lyne, in Greater Manchester. As for Heptonstall: 'I love it.'

It seems that the old feeling of an enclosed village, very crabby towards outsiders, has all but gone. One of my own principal memories of old Heptonstall is the 'simpleton' who, for years, stood in the main street, outside Heptonstall Co-op, gesticulating at everyone or no one. He was called Ernie.

Sylvia Plath's grave used to be regularly desecrated by feminists – usually on a trip over from America – because Ted Hughes, perhaps defiantly, gave her name as 'Sylvia Plath Hughes' on the gravestone. I'm told that a stonemason in Hebden Bridge used to keep replacement letters ready for when the 'Hughes' part was chipped off. All that hostility, also, seems to have faded. The grave is surprisingly neglected-looking.

Has the Elmet Trust been falling down on the job? Standing there, it strikes me that to tend the grave of the mother of Ted Hughes's two children would seem at least as important as having a Calder High School performance space named as the 'Ted Hughes Theatre'. But I must beware crabbiness. I was delighted, years back, when I was asked to give out the school prizes in this same performance space. And I like to I think my name is still included, in (perhaps flaking) gilt, on an alumni board somewhere within the school.

The Plath grave has bare earth, with a couple of plastic figurines stuck into it. A flower container is held up by a ball pen. A little lantern is filled with tiny scraps of visitors' poems. The little local museum at the edge of the graveyard displays some Ted Hughes memorabilia, but if there was anything about Sylvia Plath I missed it.

I go down and ring the doorbell at the flats. I am let in by Silly's partner. She is a pleasant, motherly young woman called Rachel Trewartha. From the name, she must be related to the Trewarthas I knew in Mytholmroyd. As we shake hands, I cite this distant link as a sort of credential. The television is on. Rachel's young daughter Ella is playing in front of it.

Silly comes in. He is thin and worn-looking. He holds himself stiffly, like an ex-soldier or an ex-alcoholic – and he is both. He comes and sits at the table next to me. We both drink Nescafé. I can't call him by his nickname. We have never met before and it sounds offensive. We agree to settle for 'Michael'. He isn't working, he tells me. He has been in prison: 'What kind of job would I get, with my record? Now I'm chief child-minder. It's t'best job in the world.' He grins. Rachel also smiles. I get the impression that she sees Michael as her 'project', but that is my word, not hers. Ella carries on playing, next to the television. Rachel turns the sound down so that we can talk better.

Looking back at the film, Michael thinks he 'upset the applecart a bit', and seems happy enough at that. As for the drinkers in the park, I'm sorry to hear him produce the old complaint that 'there's nothing for children to do'. I ask him: 'Was there ever?' I don't remember anything much being laid on for Hebden children when I grew up. It was a source of wonder and astonishment – and, for parents, regret – when an early milk bar with jukebox opened in an empty Hebden Bridge shop: Nickie's Caff. That was about it. But it *is* true that, for all the restraints of living in a village, the rules about family life and getting on with a paid job were still extremely clear.

When I suggest that liberty and freedom are not always synonymous, Michael agrees. He regrets the passing of the long-dead mills, which 'employed a lot of people'. It was mostly semi-skilled or unskilled work. You learnt on the job. You didn't have to come bearing diplomas. You had your place. At one level, meritocracy has broken all that. At another level, it has left a disaffected minority. 'It's very hard to find well-paid, full-time work,' as Michael says.

Rachel worked for a while at Mitchell mill, which Polly Webber helped to re-open. Despite the firm's hippyish past, she found that making juggling equipment was still 'boring factory work. I only did it out of necessity.' The year before we meet she'd begun an access course at Calderdale College in Halifax, in the hope of going on to a university to study for a job in social work or probation. But it was 'very hard going'. She has decided it isn't for her. She is now intending to take a college course in hairdressing.

Whatever his troubles, Michael feels a sense of comfort, he says, when he 'gets off the train in West Yorkshire, even in Bradford, and can say, "I'm home". It's where you know people, as if you've lived here all your life.' Maybe so, but both he and Rachel also say they feel 'excluded' – not welcome by everyone. Rachel makes a couple of roll-ups, lights one for herself and gives the other to Michael. 'I live off fags and coffee now,' he says.

Rachel complains about 'all the little clicks and clubs'. (I remember my mother making the same remark about tennis between the wars.) 'You feel everyone is looking down at you,' she says. 'Walking around with Ella, you get the impression people think you shouldn't be here. They think you're just council house riffraff.' 'It's more question of money,' Michael says.

He left school at sixteen and went on a jobs scheme to train as a mechanic. After that, he went to work at a friend's damp-proofing firm. He decided, next, that he'd like to join the Royal Marines, but he got impatient at the slow selection process. He went over to Calais, to join the Foreign Legion. He looked in at a *gendarmerie,* thinking that this was all he had to do. But they sent him on to the legion's recruiting office in Lille. He was accepted and did the usual gruelling training. He went on to serve in French Guiana, Djibouti and the first Gulf War. 'I'm very proud of my time in the legion. It was the best thing I ever did.' But home re-asserted its pull. He didn't sign up again.

Back in England, it was a miscellany of jobs. 'I was an insurance underwriter. Then I was living with a girlfriend on a farm. I bought a shop up Sowerby [another of the Calder valley's hilltop hamlets] and that worked for a bit. I did some forestry when the shop wasn't going well.' By then he was married and his wife was pregnant. Everything fell apart. He became a heroin addict and he partly financed the addiction through petty theft. Hence his time in prison. At one point, he was living in a tent. He broke his back and now gets incapacity benefit.

Alcohol took over from heroin. 'The dependency tied you down so much that I thought I'd prefer to be in jail. I'd be homeless, yet I'd be down at the shop in Hebden Bridge, waiting for them to open at 6.30, to buy cans of drink. It got so that they wouldn't sell it to me so early.

'When I drink, I don't just drink, I drink to get drunk. I liked being drunk. It would be best for me to go and sit in a field, if the need came over me again. Many local people won't accept that there's a huge problem. They are in denial. In the park we'd say "We're not harming anybody. Welcome to Hebden Bridge, the home of alcoholic children." Hebden has been free and easy – anything goes – you wear a poncho, with nothing on your feet.' The police mostly left them alone on the park, he says. 'We'd police it a bit for them. One of them said "If only you could put your energy to good use."' Both he and Rachel say that, even now, dealers operate next to the children's playground in the park.

Michael went along to one of the Picture House showings of Jez Lewis's film. 'I felt awful. I was drunk all day. I didn't really want to go; I had my coat on in case I was asked to leave. I'm not a dickhead. People know me.' The cinema was packed. 'A very mixed audience,' Rachel says. She listens patiently to Michael's story, breaking off from time to time to see to Ella.

He went into detox, 'but it's not been easy'. Rachel nods agreement. One day she realised he'd been back on the park, drinking. They were due to catch a bus to Halifax. When they got on, he claimed he'd only had one drink. This exasperated her and she whacked him with her handbag. The bus stopped. Someone had rung the police. It was Rachel who got arrested, for causing a disturbance. They both smile at the idiocy of it.

In spite of lapses, 'I've got faith that it will work out,' Michael says. 'And so have I,' Rachel adds. 'I now feel I have to set a good example,' he says. The Heptonstall primary school hasn't yet taken him up on his offer to 'talk to the kids about life beyond heroin'.

In the flat, Michael sees himself as being in 'a kind of cocoon'. They don't go out much. 'We shop online. It's cheaper.' He never sees his mother or any other family. He takes medication for liver disease. 'I have memory problems. I forget what day it is, and I can keep repeating myself.'

Rachel parlayed her way into this flat. She had been in a maisonette on the Dodnaze estate. 'The housing association got fed up with me complaining.' The maisonette was damp and she didn't like the neighbours. These days, Dodnaze is an estate very visibly divided into 'rough' and 'respectable'. The housing association transferred Rachel. At Heptonstall she is happy. 'I always wanted to live up here. I never thought I'd be able to.'

Michael and Rachel share, deep down, many of the values of Hebden locals. They think, for example, that many of the people on the harder drugs 'are not from round here'. They regret that children 'spend far too much time watching television'. Inevitably, as they say this, I glance at what Ella is doing. 'Oh, that's just for now,' Rachel says.

We all smile. I thank them for letting me come in. We shake hands. I like both of them. I wish them luck, and I mean it.

# 17. WORDS

In Hebden now you hardly hear any Yorkshire dialect at all. By this I
don't mean Yorkshire accents. There are plenty of those – though with
the influx of graduates and other professionals, not as many as there used
to be. The accents can be very specific. There is a certain flat combination of vowels and tones which mean that, hearing them, you can make
a good guess that the speaker comes from somewhere between Bradford
(always pronounced 'Bratford') and the Lancashire border. That is,
within a dozen miles' radius from Halifax – which includes Hebden. A
south Pennine accent, if you will.

The closer you get to Lancashire, the more you find tinges of Lancs-
speak. For example, the Yorkshire word for a narrow alley between
houses is a *ginnel*; the Lancashire word is *snicket*. In the *Hebden Bridge
Times* a letter-writer got very worked up about people using *ginnel* in a
right-of-way dispute. It was taken as proof that the users were offcomers.
A miniature language war. My own recollection is of both words being
used indiscriminately, with no comment for or against. They were syno-
nyms. The sharpest sign of an outsider would be to say *alley* or *passage*.
No one ever did.

Once acquired, a voice's local sound rarely fades away altogether.
Nor do all aspects of the dialect. A BBC studio engineer, recording my
script for a Radio 4 documentary, once suggested to my producer that the
whole thing should be re-recorded because I kept pronouncing 'us' as *uz*.
I had never even realised that it was pronounced any other way. This is
evidence, I'm sure, of my faulty ear for languages. The Radio 4 decision
was 'That's the way he speaks,' and the recording was let stand. My way

of speaking is a layered mixture of southern and northern. By now the southern is predominant, but the northern never goes away. Radio or telephone seems to bring out the northern tones more strongly.

My daughter rang, one day, to say she'd seen me on television. This surprised me. I'd not been in a studio recently. Pressing the zapper, I found that BBC2 had included a clip from a design programme I'd made about twenty-five years before. What amazed me in the clip was my cut-glass way of speaking. This hasn't lasted, unadulterated. Partly it's the passage of time. Partly it's because I thought that radio speech had changed. I deliberately roughened the edges – if that's a phrase you can use of cut glass.

Apart from that fragment of direct action, I'm not quite sure how these various changes of voice happened. As a child I spoke a broad version of Yorkshire. My mother, whose speech was much less broad than my father's, was sometimes bothered by this. When I was about six or seven, I remember she picked me up for saying *ellus* – which is Yorkshire for *always*. (It's sometimes spelled *allus*.) 'You'll grow up to be called Ellis Barker.' Ellis was an example of the local habit of using surnames for boys' Christian names. It kept you well away from any taint of saints. I knew a man called Riley Greenwood and another called Barker Clegg. I've been told of one local man who was christened Greenwood Greenwood.

In the Yorkshire dialect there are special forms of syntax, not just differences of vocabulary or pronunciation. For example, in standard English, the shortened version of 'give it to him' is 'give him it'. In Yorkshire dialect, it is 'give it him'. So far, I have never managed to thoroughly disentangle the two datives. I use each version at random. I'd guess that this muddle is now likely to continue.

Even in my childhood, the stronger forms of dialect were only used by the people who lived 'on the tops' – that is, who came down, to school or work, from the hillside farms and hamlets. Up near the moors, 'Where's ta bahn?' was likely to produce the answer 'Wom.' ('Where are you going/off to?' 'Home.') The use of variants on *thee* and *thou* was widespread. It implied some degree of intimacy: 'Don't thee thou me' was the comeback if the intimacy wasn't wanted. I've always suspected that the persistence of *thee* and *thou* related to Methodist usage in prayers and even sermons.

Some words evolved differently, north and south. In Hebden, if a child looked *starved*, this meant 'frozen'. In southern English, it means 'ill-fed'. 'Starve' comes from the same linguistic root as the German word *sterben* – which means 'to die'. The north country and the south country must have taken different views on the likeliest risk of death.

Was a mill *playing*? This meant it had shut down, probably for the wakes week holiday in mid-July. If you meant 'play', in the southern sense, the Yorkshire word was *laik* (pronounced like 'lake'). So you could say: '*I were ellus laiking.*' As that shows, verbs were declined differently. 'Was' was hardly ever used; 'were' was both singular and plural. The negative form of 'I am' was 'I a'n't' (pronounced like 'aren't') or 'I ammut' – not 'I'm not.' 'I a'n't' had been a good standard English usage, in fact – but obsolescent or long forgotten. When my sister went to work in a solicitor's office in Halifax, she tells me she was asked not to speak so 'ungrammatically'. She switched to 'I'm not.' By such erosions does dialect disappear.

In his study, *Does Accent Matter?*, the linguist John Honey pointed out that, however much it may be denied, there is a hierarchy of British regional accents. The implicit classification became especially important for British broadcasters once commercial television was introduced in 1956. The force for change was the commercial break. The old-style 'BBC' or 'Queen's English' accent – Honey and other linguists call it RP (received pronunciation) – risked making it sound as if you were talking down to consumers. Yet you still needed to be easily understood, and to carry authority alongside intimacy. In more recent years, inverted snobbery, especially the fashion for Estuary English (an Essex suburban version of Cockney), may have shifted the balance a little since Honey wrote. But not by much, and probably not for ever.

This is the 'order of acceptability' – ranked from most to least – which Honey reported, from his and other specialists' linguistic studies:

| | |
|---|---|
| 1 | Mainstream RP |
| 2 | Educated Scottish |
| 3 = | Educated Irish |
| 3 = | Educated Welsh |
| 4 = | Northern, 'with Yorkshire generally high' |

| 4 = | West Country |
|---|---|
| 5 = | London (Cockney) |
| 5 = | Liverpool (Scouse) |
| 5 = | Glaswegian |
| 5 = | West Midlands (Brummie) |

If you included Northern Ireland accents, Honey reported, they ranked in category 5. Asian and Caribbean accents also ranked low. So did 'extreme' RP, which I suppose you could call toff-speak.

Yorkshire wasn't down at the bottom of the list, alongside Brummie or Glaswegian. But the message for anyone hoping to get on in the world was then, and remains now, pretty clear. This is why the answer to 'Who pronounces *butcher* with a light 'u' as in *much*?' is always: 'a politely spoken Yorkshirewoman'. The lesson that broad u's are unacceptable can be over-learnt. The mill owner's wife who, at Sunday school, tried to teach me the lessons of the Bible – a task on which she battled away bravely, sometimes over tea – spoke like this.

In inner London now, you hear some black children speaking a revived version of Jamaican patois, incomprehensible to anyone but themselves. This is the mode of speech that their parents and grand-parents, as immigrants, tried to move away from (though, as with my residual *uz*, the Caribbean pronunciation *aks*, instead of *ask*, proved very hard to shift). There is no parallel move in Hebden or, so far as I know, anywhere else in Yorkshire, to revive the Yorkshire dialect.

When I reached the sixth form and was beginning to wonder about applying for university entrance, my mother booked me in at weekly speech classes in Halifax. I don't know how she found out about them. I was against the idea, but not so hostile that I refused to go. The classes mostly consisted of reciting poems you'd chosen to bring with you. Pretentiously, I made T.S. Eliot my star turn. I had just been bowled over by his poetry. I'm not sure how many of my fellow-students appreciated Eliot's reworking of Lancelot Andrewes's words, in 'The Journey of the Magi', as much as I did: 'A cold coming we had of it,/ Just the worst time of the year/ For a journey. . . .' Eliot could have been describing the experience of catching a corporation bus into Halifax in January.

I kept very quiet in Hebden about these classes, which I think lasted only a few months. Nor can they have been all that successful. A friend from Surrey remembers me from when we turned up together to seek admission to college. He claims he had never before heard a Yorkshire accent – in life, I suppose, as opposed to on the radio. He reports that I said that something or other was 'right grand', with all the proper Yorkshire vowels.

These speech habits all eroded – so far as I can now tell – by then spending two conscripted years in the army, all of it in the south of England and almost entirely among southerners. Osmosis, rather than erosion. Three years at university probably finished the job. But the process must have been so gradual that I could never tell exactly how or when it took place. Nor was I conscious of trying to do anything about it. And nor, in the end, was the process ever completed.

Dialect aside, the old ways enwrapped the Hebden I grew up in. At the right season, we children got out our whips and tops. We played elaborate games with marbles along the pavement edge. The school play-ground was chalked out for hopscotch. There was another playground game, which I think was called 'Thrush'. This was a version of leapfrog. You had to jump as far over a line of crouched boys as you could. And they had to withstand it. (The Opies reported dozens of alternative local names, nationwide, for this game. Hi Jimmy Knacker was the common-est.) Playgrounds were divided into 'boys' and 'girls'. Thrush was 100 per cent male. The girls, after all, had their skipping ropes – which were 100 per cent female. Blue Milk was a version of tag ('tig', in Yorkshire), in which girls were not specifically excluded, but in practice never took part.

Nor did girls play Kick-Can. For this, you put an old tin can where two or three streets joined. All the players dispersed but one, who had to catch any of the rest from getting as far as the can and kicking it. Surprisingly, no neighbours ever complained. They had probably done the same thing as children. Nor do I remember anyone complaining about Mischief Night – 4 November, the day before Bonfire Night. Door knobs were tied to dustbin lids, or even two adjacent front-doors tied together, before you knocked or rang and retreated to see and hear the noisy outcome.

All this has been overtaken by the transatlantic importation of trick-or-treat and other Hallowe'en formulas. (Methodists and Evangelicals have done their horrified best to halt the Hallowe'en craze, with no success.) Hebden – inevitably? – also has a strong contingent of pagans, for whom Bonfire Night and Halloween are only latecomer variants on the supposed ancient festival of Samhaim.

Margaret Murray, the anthropologist who invented the pagan 'ancient religion' of Wicca in her 1921 book, *The Witch Cult in Western Europe*, has a lot to answer for. But beliefs ebb and flow. There are, for example, no 'Particular Baptists' left in Hebden Bridge. Their huge chapel, with its own special rites, was for decades kept going by a single surviving member. Like so many chapels, it is now divided into flats. But Hebden has plenty of pagans.

More pagans now, I'd bet, than Trotskyites. From about 1975 to about 1990, astringent critiques of late capitalism used to flourish round every corner in Hebden. I sat in on some of the early meetings and found it hard to stay awake. Such dogmas have gone the way of the Communist Party member, from the now-demolished slums of Garden Street, who persistently to tried to sell copies of the party's *Daily Worker* to the Saturday night second-house queue at the Picture House. I never saw anyone buy a copy.

Like all religious sects, in Hebden or elsewhere, paganism splinters into numerous sub-sects. Bookcase, the longest-established Hebden Bridge bookshop, has a good supply of rival texts. Paganism seems to shade off into a belief in ghosts and all varieties of the paranormal. In the National Trust car park at Hardcastle Crags, I see a bright yellow Fiat Seicento, with an amber roof-flasher like an emergency service. The car describes itself as from the 'Hull Paranormal Society: you can visit us online'. The car's occupants have gone off walking, so I never find out what the emergency is. Not enough ghosts in Hebden? Too many?

# 18. GRAVES

Jack Greenwood was the caretaker and sexton of Slack chapel. He lived in a little cottage overlooking the cemetery. It was his *job* to dig the graves. It was his *passion* to keep an eye on what was going on all around. The cemetery was high above Hardcastle Crags, on a windswept hillside. When I interviewed him, in the late 1970s, he had 280 graves to look after.

'I have th'advantage over anyone who'd do this job. I served eight year under my great-uncle who were t'sexton here for forty-two year. It's a funny thing to explain. As a young lad I were knocking around wi' old men, the youngest about seventy, and they used to come to t'cemetery during t'day and I hadn't to speak – ask no questions. And it used to be that usual topic: "Who're you burying today, John?" And in t'next few minutes you got all that person's history. Those little things, when you came to do the job, they're a great help, I can tell you.

'The amount of John Sutcliffes, John Green'uds [Greenwoods], William Green'uds: you had to sort 'em out, which of 'em it were, if you hadn't knowledge of their by-names, such as John o'Pharoah's [a farm], Jack o'Nancy's, Jack o'Betty's. You generally got just "John Greenwood". As he named names, he gestured down the cemetery to where those men lay.

Sometimes there was confusion. 'It took me into t'teens o' meetings with t'chapel treasurer, a very stubborn man, to find where half o' t'graves were. It should all have been on a map. There were entries on the register and minute books that made better reading nor [than] *Lady Chatterley*. So particular in detail – how somebody died, that sort of thing. The details might do somebody some good, they thought, in years to come.

'You had weekly and monthly meetings of t'chapel committee, and it were brought in front o' t'committee about a certain lady that had been misbehaving. And they proposed that she be brought in front of them to toe the line. They did so. And she said she would. You read on, and later in t'same year – same thing again. So they propose that they delegate three committee members to visit her at home – the minister, a lady and a man. They were to meet at t'manse. The man was missing. The other two went on the visit. As they were leaving the woman's house, the woman who lived next door but one came out and said "Where's our Jim?" They said they hadn't seen him. "He's wi' you," she said. But they said "Jim weren't for going." It turned out he were one o' t'lady's lovers.'

They were tough people around here. 'Betty Nine-Coats lived t'other side o' Popples [a big field near the chapel]. They sent someone across to see if she needed help. They'd heard she'd fallen on hard times. She slammed t'door in their face, and never went to t'chapel again till they buried her. And it's in t'minute book.'

The cemetery was now owned by the Yorkshire Baptist Association at Leeds, he said. So they're your bosses? 'Nay, I haven't onny.' A very Hebden remark. The undertakers paid Jack by the job. He was sixty-five. 'I more or less gave a promise to th'older members of the congregation that I'd carry on. I didn't think it were playing the game to say "That's it." There are some families with only one or two left, and have been looking forward to joining their relatives – aiming towards that. I'll carry on for that reason.'

His own family had almost always lived in the house by the cemetery, he said. It used to be a corn chandler's, and still had a first-floor outside door for the sacks. The corn was mostly for hens. 'There used to be twenty or thirty hen huts on Popples, right up till World War Two. Nearly every family had their hut. People had two jobs. Farmers made some extra money by mill work, council work, even road sweeper.

'I've lived within sight of that chapel all my life. I've three married sons, two of them in Hebden Bridge. The oldest has the butcher's shop on Market Street.' Jack went to school at Heptonstall. 'I remember a painting lesson. Fruit were in season. We was asked to bring some. Twenty pupils and six blackberries each. At playtime, the teacher said, 'Leave t'specimens on t'desk, next to t'painting. After, t'painting was there, but t'blackberries had gone.'

He was christened Jack 'because there were three Johns in t'family'. His father's by-name was Jim o'Rob's – that is, James, son of Robert Greenwood. Jack left school at thirteen and started at Ormerods light engineering works in Hebden Bridge. When Ormerods went bankrupt, 'there were no jobs going then. I started helping t'old chap here.' He did eventually get a job at F&H Sutcliffe's, the firm by the railway station which made greenhouses and other kinds of shed.

An uncle of mine, who'd trained as a cabinet-maker, went there when work was short, and stayed for the rest of his life. 'F&Hs' weren't known for their skilled work. The joke was that 'an F&H screwdriver' was a hammer. I did a summer job there, one year. The big deal was 'the WC rota', which gave men time to sit and work out their horse-racing bets. 'F&H's ellus wanted men when there were work,' Jack said. 'When there weren't work, then you were out. But t'last time they didn't get chance to sack me. I sacked meself. HK [the boss] didn't like it, but he got it, and I came here.'

Jack remembered without any fondness the people who thought of themselves as local gentry. 'Gamaliel Sutcliffe, himself he used to say "You'll see t'Sutcliffe family i'clogs", and it's come to it. Gamaliel were a big local figure, a big house at Slack, a typical country squire. The family came from up Crimsworth. He were a poor landlord. I remember t'funeral. Schoolchildren were all lined up. As a child, you had to raise your cap if you met the Sutcliffe coach and horses. But you took good care not to meet them – because, if you forgot to raise your cap, you heard about it, or your parents did. They had a tremendous staff and it's all come to nothing, as you might say. It was thought that there were some things only a Sutcliffe could do. Gamaliel's grave is at the foot of Heptonstall church tower, with railings round. There's only one Sutcliffe left who can authorise it to be oppened. What'll happen after it's oppened up for him? But it's a stipulation. One of the Sutcliffe heirs was disowned. He'd married a black woman.'

Abraham Gibson was another who was the last in a long local family line: the Gibsons of the eighteenth-century Gibson mill in Hardcastle

Crags. 'Ab was a comical character. He could never get it into his head that times were changing. The only close company he ever had in his big house at Slack were old people – his mother and the housekeeper. He never married. His mother brought him, every Sunday, to Slack chapel in the morning and Heptonstall church at night. She'd hold his hand and he were thirty years old, nearly. He kept his childhood cradle in his bedroom. After Ab's death, there were a big sale o' things and property. Most of the money went to Heptonstall church.

'When undertakers come,' Jack said, 'there's no need now to look at records to find where folk are. I know where they are. But I look into t'register, just to make sure. It's force of habit. If you were digging there, in that corner, you'd know nearly every word on that stone when you'd finished. You gradually get to know them, all round t'cemetery.'

Cremations, which usually took place in Halifax, meant that 'you can go a month here, and there's nowt'. In between times, he used to deliver coal and groceries for Heptonstall Co-op, till it closed. Then Hebden Bridge Co-op. Then he helped out for the coal merchant, Matthew Sheard.

'They always say, "There's nowt queerer nor folk," and there was never a truer word spoken. Farmers up Crimsworth are still in t'year dot, like Charlie and his sister Sarah Hannah at Thurrish. Old-fashioned. They'll never get out of it. But they accept you. I suppose it's summat, to be accepted by someone.' He laughed.

'In my mother's day, when you went to chapel, your job was more or less secured. Mill owners were on t'chapel committee. Your parents worked for them, and so did you. At Slack we had t'cream o' t'manufacturers: Richard Sutcliffe, treasurer; Sutcliffe Pickles, Sunday school superintendant; Miss Emily Sutcliffe, head teacher; Sam Marshall and Abraham Marshall. All t'big men were up here. When they buried Roger Shackleton – that red grave there – they had tea in t'Sunday school for 170. And they buried his wife here, and his son. They're all Shackletons in this corner. For Roger's funeral, they had all the front of the chapel laid out like a garden. All t'bedding plants were given, after t'funeral, to various people that had attended. Members o' t'tea committee belonging to t'chapel officiated, and t'caretaker. They all got £5 each.

'A lot o' things were done then that there weren't any need for it. The wearing of mourning died out after World War Two. At the same time, local undertakers gave up wearing t'crape on t'long hat.

'When you've been in this job a long, long while, you form in your own mind what type of funeral affects people most. The only ones I don't want to do are a child, knocked down by a car or whatever. You just have to do your job, and keep an eye on t'family in case anyone collapses. I had some ashes sent from America direct to me. The man died at ninety-three. He'd been a teacher at Heptonstall school. I buried his brother. It's surprising how many come back, from such a wide area. They always counted on it being home, in some way. You don't know where t'next job is coming from. That man there is from Ashton-in-Makerfield [in Greater Manchester]. If they can't be side by side with their family, they'll be opposite. As if they want to get as near as they can.

'A married couple are buried there, under t'wall. Same name as you, but it's a Heptonstall Barker.' In fact, various relatives on my mother's side – that is, none of them a Barker – are buried here. But I don't want to go into all that with Jack. 'That couple died within a week of one another and wanted to be buried facing one another. We got t'coffins in, but we had to turn 'em on t'side.'

'Folk have these little bits o' fancies. Fred Barker's wife, she had to be buried in her best silk dress and her jewellery. Well, what good is it? But you couldn't tell her so. It makes you stop and think. I've one woman buried there, under that tree. She'd written about this grave, it were her parents' grave. It were bricked in wi' flags on top ['flags' are the large flat stones for pavements or graves]. When you're down there, you can hear the slightest noise. It's 15 foot to t'bottom. After the burial, I heard a funny noise, tap, tap, tap.' He raps the table we're sitting at. 'I mentioned it to my son. "Had she a watch on?" he asked. It turned out she had an eight-day wristwatch on. She must have wound it up the same night she died. She had her hand touching the coffin lid.'

He laughed. 'My son said, "It's valuable, it's valued at 40 quid." But she said we wasn't to take that watch off, under no consideration. So we didn't do.'

# 19. LARKS

Jack Ingham, by-name 'Larky', said he used to breed skylarks for singing contests and for keeping as cage birds. Recorded in the 1970s, he said: 'You caught them young and fed 'em. You put 'em in a cage with a cloth on top, to stop them trying to rise. The hens, you released. The cocks, you put them in a dark box, for learning 'em to sing. You entered them for singing contests. For a copper kettle prize. Everything were for a copper kettle i' them days. Lark-catching for contests is illegal now, and has been for many a year.'

He lived at Midgley, one of the hamlets up above Mytholmroyd. The big employer for Midgley people was Murgatroyds' Oats Royd woollen mill in the Luddenden side-valley. The mill was enormous, with a high bridge arching across the road to link the two halves together. At its peak, Oats Royd employed 2,000 people. It met its end in February 1989, with a stupendous fire. The classic mill family saga, Thomas Armstrong's *The Crowthers of Bankdam* (1940; filmed in 1947 as *The Master of Bankdam*, with Dennis Price and Tom Wall), fitted Oats Royd and the Murgatroyds like a glove. Upstream from the mill, the Murgatroyds lived part of the time at Castle Carr, a Victorian Gothic folly. The Fieldens had already built Dobroyd Castle for themselves, up above Todmorden. Anything you can do, I can do better?

Nestling in the Luddenden valley, Castle Carr was as gloomy as something out of *Jane Eyre* or *Wuthering Heights*. The grounds opened to the public once a year (and still do). You could walk across the hill from Mytholmroyd for a picnic. On the way you passed Churn Milk Joan, a tall stone pillar in the middle of the moor. Children were held up to put a penny or two in a hollow at the top, for good luck. No one quite knew what Churn Milk Joan was for – perhaps a boundary marker. Tales are spun about who 'Joan' was. In truth, it is as unexplained as Abel Cross in the Crimsworth valley. Today there is little evidence of Castle Carr. It was pulled down, and the stone sold, after 100 years. After the fire, what was left of Oats Royd was partly demolished, partly converted into flats. No one wept for the departure of the Murgatroyds.

Jack Ingham used to be a beater for the Murgatroyd grouse shoots. 'I were a turner-in, driving t'grouse towards t'butts. Afterwards, I'd pick up pennies the shooters had thrown down.' He was also a poacher. 'Murgatroyd at Castle Carr offered me wine after I said I wouldn't pull walls down in hunting for rabbits. But I was fined £1, one time, for coneying.' ('Coney', now extinct outside dialect, is a much older word than 'rabbit'.)

There were rival poachers: 'We had some right good gang fights. Murgatroyd wouldn't have any guns on t'moor. Tha had to have a good dog, and then you'd be right. I spent many a hundred hours rabbiting. But there were shoots of live pigeons – and also of sparrows. There'd be pigeon pie and sparrow pie afterwards. Shepsters [starlings] were also put into pies and were well thought of. There were a lot more meat on them than on sparrows.'

Jack's memories were recorded by Peggy Horsfield, who lived at a farm in Midgley, to mark the hundredth anniversary, in 1997, of Midgley school. Like all the upper Calder valley schools, including Burnley Road school in Mytholmroyd and Heptonstall school, this began life as a 'board school', taking all children except the few who transferred to grammar school, right up to the school-leaving age of thirteen (part-time from eleven for many boys). Now they are all primary schools, but at a glance, with their solid, adaptable Victorian architecture, they still look much the same.

Midgley is where, in the 1930s, a version of the Easter-tide 'Pace Egg' play was woven together by two of the schoolmasters. It had previously existed in shortened forms – for performing for pennies from street to street. My father, who was always good at extempore one-liners, played Old Tosspot, the main comedian in the play. The hero is St

9. On this day in 1977 my family and I sat in the sun by the edge of the Crimsworth stream. On the moors beyond, as a teenager, I helped beat for grouse. A young man came hopping down the middle of the stream, clicking his camera. He turned out to be the photographer Martin Parr, not long out of Manchester art school, now living in Hebden Bridge. It seemed we were part of a project to record the British at leisure. Next day I picked up this print. Left to right: our son Nicholas reading; my father in his summery hat; my wife Sally; our youngest son Daniel in the stream; our daughter Kate next to him; me looking down towards Sally; and Tom, our other son, looking thoughtful.

LEFT 10. *The very image of self-help. In his Hebden years, Martin Parr tried to capture every aspect of 1970s life. I ought to know this man, cleaning the transom of his door in 1976, and the street he's on. Both are now lost in the mists of memory.*

RIGHT AND BELOW 11 *and* 12. *The new Hebden at play. The annual Handmade Parade is organised by an admirable set-up called Thingumajig Theatre. Run by Andrew Kim and Kathy Bradley, it's based in an old chapel. The Thingumajig work-room is a brightly hued puppetry treasure house. The puppets that star in the parade are like friendly giants. Above: a huge, glittery Queen Bee crosses a canal bridge. Below: Thingumajig's very friendly dragon, Veronica, meets a crowd of her admirers.*

ABOVE 13 *and* 14. *For the putative 500th anniversary of Hebden Bridge in 2010, the designer Mike Barrett decided that the phrase 'It's So Hebden Bridge' said it all. He put it on the anniversary brochures (above) and on big signposts as you came into Hebden Bridge or (above right) sped away.*

RIGHT 15. *Post-industrial Hebden Bridge probably sees art and industry as opposites. The local Little Theatre, founded in 1924, thought that each could gain from the other. Its Art Deco logo 'Art Rising from Industry' shows the muse of drama against a backdrop of mills. I saw my first-ever Molière play in this theatre, which still flourishes.*

16. *A worker in the Moderna blanket factory, Mytholmroyd, in 1977, not long before it closed. Portrayed by Daniel Meadows. My father worked in this factory. He liked it, but saw no future in his job. The firm believed in treating workers well. In its heyday, it had its own brass band.*

17. *At Lady Willie's restaurant, a group of women, who'd been to the grammar school together, met for a yearly high tea. My mother-in-law, Marion Huddleston (née Ashworth), is fourth from the left in the back row. The photographer, Alice Longstaff, is at the far left, having set her camera-timer. For decades, she took studio portraits and covered special events. She also took photograph after photograph, chronicling the changing town. Images all now held in a special Alice Longstaff Collection.*

18. *Hippie days. The Queen's Terrace squat, protesting against threatened demolition, was a turning point. The bulldozers stayed away. The terrace is still there. No more old, perfectly usable houses were pulled down.*

19. *A perfect picture of old Hebden. Martin Parr became fascinated by the old farms and chapels along the Crimsworth valley. This is the Harvest Festival at Pecket Well chapel, 1978. The face of the man leaning forward says 'Yorkshire' in every lineament. The man to the left is Stanley Greenwood, of White Hole farm, who lent me his list of Greenwood 'by-names'. The chapel is now a house; its Sunday school made over into flats. The Co-op and chapel culture is dead.*

20. *It all comes back to the landscape. Fay Godwin took this photograph for the cover of* Remains
of Elmet. *This book places her Hebden landscape photographs alongside specially written poems by
Mytholmroyd-born Ted Hughes. (My aunt Marjorie, who lived on the same street, always called him
'young Teddy'.) Heptonstall church is on the hilltop beyond the valley of the river Hebden. On a further
hill you see the obelisk of Stoodley Pike. When I rented a cottage for research on this book, the view from
the terrace was almost identical with this.*

George. When the Pace Egg was a living tradition, the words were not sacred. Nor did anyone think of it as *acting*. The snatches of doggerel dialogue which *had* been handed down were declaimed or recited, like a child's lesson, in as loud a voice as possible.

As edited, and now performed by Calder High School pupils, it seems like an interminable piece of half-fake folklorism, with everyone acting away like mad. Perhaps inevitably it is now seen as embodying 'the age-old struggle between good and evil'. The 'struggle' has been cleaned up. Old Tosspot no longer carries over his shoulder a floppy Tally Wife puppet. (Living 'tally' or 'over t'brush' meant cohabiting.) Unfumigated, the Pace Egg play was seen as a bit of harmless fun. Not any more. Watching the Pace Egg players may be one of the experiences that has put me off seeing morris dancing, if I can avoid it. Another solemn and unlovely bit of revivalism.

Why Midgley? Like Heptonstall – which has its own version of Pace Egg – it was far enough off the beaten track for customs to survive there longer than elsewhere. 'Colloping', for example, was recorded by Peggy Horsfield at Midgley. It took place on Collop Monday, which was the day before Shrove Tuesday ('Pancake Day'). The three Farrar sisters, then all in their nineties, told Peggy that children went round 'colloping' at different houses, 'begging for a collop [a slice] o' bacon. They wanted the fat for pancakes on the Tuesday.'

Peggy's great-great-grandfather had lived in the house where I went to see her. Peggy's family name was Crowther, and her father was out haymaking on the farm as we spoke. In Midgley, when she grew up, almost the only jobs apart from Oats Royd mill and the farms were in the quarries on the moor edge. The Midgley social scale, she said, was: 'Murgatroyds; then professional people – teachers, clergymen and such-like; then quarry owners; then farmers and tradespeople; then mill hands; then workers in the stone quarries.'

The Crowthers were farmers. But her husband's family were quarry workers – a couple of social pegs down. Peggy's father had hoped to break away from Midgley, and become a professional singer. He left Midgley school to train at the Royal Manchester College of Music, but it 'faded off'. He then came back to Hebden Bridge grammar school and helped on his father's farm.

'Murgatroyds owned a lot of land and farms,' Peggy said. 'People looked up to them. There's only one Murgatroyd left now, and he's not a Murgatroyd in name. It was Murgatroyds' till Mr Ronald died two years ago. It is no longer a family firm. It was taken over. Rows and rows of houses have been pulled down, originally built by Murgatroyds for their workers, some of them were back-to-back. A lot of old farmhouses were also pulled down. Even in the heyday, people who farmed usually worked in the mill as well. The children would help take the cans of milk out on the way to school and collect them on the way home.'

Peggy's father was one of those who bought some Murgatroyd land. At its largest, their farm was about 50 acres. When we spoke, it was about 12 acres, with twenty milk cows and calves, poultry and pigs. 'Only two local farmers now produce milk and deliver it themselves,' she said. 'The rest sell to dairies, who deliver. World War Two ended village life as it used to be. Conscription broadened people's outlook, then cars. And there was the shortage of work around here. People decided they preferred town life to country life, I suppose.

'Greenwoods and Horsfields, those were Midgley names. When business was good, people came from Liverpool and the north-east to work at Murgatroyds, also the Irish, maybe via Liverpool.

'The chapel, the Co-op, the mill and the quarry: they were the four important aspects of village life. Midgley was a flourishing Co-op. It always paid a good dividend or whatever. Sowerby Co-op was in a bad way. They bought Midgley to try to recover themselves, and they didn't, and the whole lot went. The butcher's and the cloggers had closed beforehand, but the drapery, the groceries and the coal carried on right till the end.

'The quarrying closed about fifteen years ago. Some quarries were used as landfill, then re-seeded. The quarry men were hard men. But one of them, John Craven, was a stalwart of the church. He was very devout and spoke in a strong, shouting voice. He spoke – very slowly – emphasising every word he said. You were impressed by his voice and his speech, rather than by what he said.'

Peggy's son was out in the fields, 'driving the tractor. He has horticulture in mind. That's what he'll go to university for, if he goes.'

# 20. HOME

No. 6 Erringden Road was (and is) a small, redbrick and pebbledash house, in the middle of a terrace of four. It was a new-built council house when my parents moved into it in 1931. My mother would have preferred one of the houses on the new estates at the edges of Mytholmroyd village, which were being offered for sale by private builders. At a time when so many people rented, my father was wary of taking on a mortgage.

Erringden Road was far from the image evoked by the words 'council house' now. It was an estate of only four streets, tucked in between private housing. Even so, there were two shadowy figures I saw walking along the pavement from time to time. The 'kid hunter' – the school attendance officer – would come to ask parents, rather forcefully, why an absent child wasn't at school. He might well take the child back, himself. And there was the 'cruelty man' – the NSPCC inspector – who would call after any complaints that a child was being ill-treated. My mother said, once, that the cruelty man had called at No. 2 Erringden Road, our next-door neighbours but one. Neither of these law enforcers called at No. 6.

Across a small garden and a narrow road, the front of our house looked out on to the railway line. When the trains were shunted, every wagon coupling clattered against the next. You hardly noticed it. Children often went up to the nearby footbridge to enjoy the smoke and steam coming up from the trains. When there seemed to be no train coming, we would creep on to the line and put a penny to be flattened. For years the only time we ever actually caught a train, as a family, was to make the annual pilgrimage to Blackpool: see the circus, go to a variety theatre every night, enjoy the slot machines at the Tower or on Central Pier, sneak a look at the postcards. But trains were part of growing up on Erringden Road.

When I was at Burnley Road school, we bought a small dog. It was meant to be 'mine', though my father had grown up with dogs. He loved them and was good at training them. Somehow the puppy got out on to the railway and was decapitated by a train. I think I shed more tears then than at any time before or since. I came down into the living room and sobbed. In those days, you had to take out a licence when a dog was six months old. The puppy hadn't reached that stage. It hadn't become 'adult'. It was a child like me. Between tears, I explained that this made its death even worse.

On one side of us, at No. 4, lived Mr Brock, the manager of the local council's sewage works. We never saw much of him. On the other side, at No. 8, lived Mr Speak. His children, Peter and Marjorie, were much older than us. Peter played the bassoon. You could hear the sound – 'like a dying cow', my father said – through the thin walls. After a stint as a Bevin Boy miner, Peter became a schoolteacher. Marjorie became a hotel receptionist – seen, then, as a good job for a girl. They were a very pleasant family and we stayed in touch after they moved a few miles away.

With them, from their new home, we walked out to where Robin Hood had supposedly been buried. The story was that, while the outlaw was lying fatally wounded in a room in Kirklees Priory, he shot an arrow out of a window with his last breath – to signal where he wanted to lie. A monument by the river Calder claimed to be his gravestone. The Speaks had a piano, and I played draughts and solitaire with them. Not chess: my father had a theory that chess drove its players mad. In the First World War, Mr Speak had been a conscientious objector, and was imprisoned (in Dartmoor, it was said). He had a hard time of it. I think he was a member of the pacifist Independent Labour Party.

At Erringden Road, our front garden was the children's garden. My sister, Elaine, and I had a sandpit. We planted marigolds and cuttings of Dorothy Perkins roses. The back garden was larger but more utilitarian. There was a shed, where I had tame mice, but they never survived for long. There were a few hens. Also, rabbits in cages which caught fatal illnesses – so we children were assured – with strange regularity. We had a steady amount of rabbit stew during the wartime and postwar rationing. Legitimately, because rabbit meat wasn't part of the rationing scheme. Nor was horse. Only later did my mother reveal that, in desperation for meat, she went into Halifax market and bought some. She never 'let on'. No one realised.

Seen now, the house looks small. It has been sold off, and the present owner has turned the front garden into a tarmacked parking space. By contrast, the back garden is now much more elaborately laid out. It is protected by a high wooden fence. To a child, the house didn't seem small. Downstairs it had a living room, a kitchen and a bathroom and lavatory; upstairs three bedrooms. This was at a time when many of the houses we visited – relatives, for example, or parents' friends – had no bathroom and still had outside lavatories. I remember the kitchen mainly as a source of treats: scraping out the remains of cake mixture from the bowl, or watching jugged pigeon being cooked when Elaine or I was ill.

The worst childhood illness was one which couldn't be mitigated this way. Elaine caught scarlet fever which, before antibiotics, was a potentially deadly infection. She was taken away by ambulance to the isolation hospital, in the former workhouse. For the six weeks she was away, she and my parents could only see one another through a glass panel.

We ate in the living room. I remember the mealtimes for two early conflicts with my father. Once I was looking at some book – the *Daily Mail* annual, I think. I should have been eating. He tore out the page I was reading and threw it on the open fire. I managed to rescue most of it. Another time, I had taken a G.K. Chesterton collection of stories out of the library. I was impressed by one of Chesterton's characteristic paradoxes: that you could bet on anything, even the speed of raindrops running down a window pane, and perhaps even God wouldn't know the answer in advance. It was raining as we ate. I watched the raindrops running down and produced my snippet of knowledge. My father was infuriated, took the book, and returned it to the library himself.

I never forgave him for these things – so small, I suppose, that nobody but me remembered them. Nor did I ever forget, or forgive, the first words I remember him ever speaking to me. A friend of his, who worked as a roadman, had seen me take refuge in a nearby darkened air-raid shelter when I was being chased by a boy who persecuted me, fairly steadily, for a year or more. The man told my father – who said to me: 'I don't want any boy of mine to be a coward.'

In *The Uses of Literacy*, Richard Hoggart wrote, plangently, about the grammar school boy from a modest background needing to cut himself off from his roots. In particular, from his family. When I read Hoggart's book, years later, I took his point. But I had never found it a problem. I was always detached.

I should make it clear that it was a happy childhood, and my mother and father were very good parents. It's just that ways of bringing up children have changed. Or, more generally, ways of being a family. In those distant Hebden days, the question, 'Is he a good husband?', meant two things, or perhaps three. Does he work hard? Does he drink? Does he hit his wife? The answers to the latter two questions were closely related. On all these points, my father was a good husband. But he was also one of those people who are light-hearted among company but much less cheerful at home. It probably didn't help that, from a young age, I would always talk back, if he said something I didn't like. He only took his belt off to me once, with me scrambling up the stairs to get out of the way, and my peacemaker mother calling out from below to try to stop all this.

What was unusual was that this only happened once. We knew of one man who used to strap his daughter until she was in her teens. In the days of caning in schools, head teachers would take care to cane their own children – if they were at the same school and broke the rules – harder than other pupils. It was the way things were. I don't think it did anybody any good.

Another side of parenting was the fear of spoiling children by over-praise. My parents followed this rule rigidly. This is hard to understand now, when the trend is the opposite: always to heap on the praise for even the tiniest achievement. In Burnley Road school, which was then organised by 'standards', not classes, I always came out top. I still have the copy of Alison Uttley's *Sam Pig Goes to Market* which the school gave me for being 'Top in Standard I' – which was the first grade above infants. None of the other children seemed to mind that I was so interminably marked out as special. The one exception was the boy who bullied me. His motive may also have been that I was one of the smallest boys for my age.

The same pattern of prizes carried on at grammar school. Every single year, I walked out on the stage of the Picture House to collect the form prize. Hebden Bridge had one of the modest local grammar schools set up by the West Riding county council in the early years of the twentieth century, as soon as they were legally empowered to spend money on secondary education. To begin with, it was called simply 'Hebden Bridge and District Secondary School.' Its second head teacher, Herbert Howarth, then introduced the Latin lessons which were required for all university admissions, and renamed it as a grammar school. Most parents paid modest fees, until the arrival of the eleven-plus in the 1940s created a hurdle which all entrants had to pass. Even so, Hebden Bridge grammar school was admitting about one third of local eleven year olds (in A or B streams) by the time it was merged into the Calder High School comprehensive.

From Hebden, a few children went to Heath grammar school in Halifax (Laurence Sterne was the best-known old boy); one or two commuted into Manchester Grammar School. A scattering of mill owners' children went to lower- or middle-rung public schools. But I knew nothing about all that then. Hebden was a world of its own. To my knowledge, in those days, class never surfaced. Even when I was drafted into being the Conservative candidate in a school mock election – not that I *was* a Conservative, then or since – I fought entirely on pastiches of Churchill's reported speeches. My Labour and Liberal opponents fought in much the same way. At those hustings, I don't remember class differences ever being mentioned. What would they mean in Hebden? Nothing much.

I am told that my parents were very proud of my achievements at school and in getting into university. But they never said so. I wasn't bothered (in the classic northern phrase). I only find it odd when I think back. That was the way it was. Going to university was, then, a very unusual event. For a few years, it was a time of extraordinary state generosity (under a Tory government, by the way). Having gained admission, I was automatically given a full, non-means-tested state scholarship, with no tuition fees and a high maintenance grant. I needn't even have gone on to take A-levels, though I did. I went to Wakefield, the West Riding county town, to be seen by the education committee. With very little ado, I was given an honorary 'county major' scholarship. I then made my first-ever trip to London, to Gordon Square in Bloomsbury, to have the state scholarship endorsed, also with little fuss.

My parents were most visibly pleased when, during my National Service, I was commissioned. They had heard so much about the Duke of Wellington's Regiment commission awarded to an Ashworth cousin of mine, the son of my mother's brother. There was always some tension between Barkers and Ashworths, a tiny sliver of social difference, as I now see it. The only parental remark I remember, after the university admission letter arrived, was my father's 'I don't expect you'll want to speak to us at all now.' I was amazed. I'd no idea what he was talking about. But there it was . . .

Hoggart writes of his shame at not being able to enjoy a drink with his father, or share a joke. Much later on, influenced by Hoggart, I tried to do something about this. My father and I would go together for a gill (a half-pint, in northern measures) at the pub opposite our Hebden Bridge house. It was all a bit strained. But, by then, we got on more or less all right. When we had a family of our own, both of my parents would come down for a holiday and to help.

Though my father had a happy life in many ways, and successfully ran three shops – first, the fish and chip shops in Mytholmroyd, and then a corner shop in Hebden Bridge – I now think of him as being deeply frustrated. Even as having a chip on his shoulder. He was a paid-up member of the awkward squad (an honourable stance, in its way). He was very bright but had almost no education to help him build on that brightness. I never saw him read a book. Unlike my mother, who liked novelists who told a clear, realistic story, such as Catherine Cookson.

Ours was a house without books, apart from Christmas-time *Beano* or *Dandy* annuals or the like. In my eyes, one great advantage of school prizes, as of Sunday school attendance prizes, was that you got a book. But what books to buy when Hebden had no bookshop, and Halifax not much of one, was always a bit of a dilemma. Does anyone need any copies of the *Empire Youth Annual*?

# 21. LIVES

IN MY FATHER'S WORDS:

'My grandfather were the overlooker, in charge of the mules at Robertshaw's Westfield Mill in Mytholmroyd. [Mules were the huge spinning frames, some with hundreds of spindles each.] He were a right bastard. There were no favouritism when I were there. On the contrary. It were his job to shut the doors. We started at six and at five past they were locked. He took great pleasure in it. Them that were late had to wait under a long shed at the side till half past eight. Then they were there to start at nine. And it was all taken off your wages. He weren't a big 'un, not much abun five foot – but he was as broad'.

My great-grandfather – Tom Harry – was also known locally for the miniature Yorkshire terriers he bred. And when his first grandson Harry, my father's eldest brother, had to go to a specialist school, Tom Harry paid. The bargee was *his* father.

'My father, your grandfather, was also at Robertshaw's, as a loom tackler [engineer]. Your uncle George were there. A man left to go to the First World War. Father said he'd do the job. It was all going to be over by Christmas, you know. He were still doing it in 1920, and got no more money. But we got lots o' turkeys from Robertshaw's out o' t'job. We were never bout a turkey at Christmas. But father upped and left to Pickles's, and George and I left as well. George went to F&H Sut's in Hebden and I went to Radcliffe's [a blanket works] in Mytholmroyd as under-tackler. Three on us in one shop was too many, any road.

'I've never been one for getting on wi' bosses. There was a teacher at Burnley Road called Baxendale. He used to hit out wi' a ruler. So we got a bit of a saw and cut half-through, so it broke. He walloped a couple on us for that. So when he were bicycling home, we hid by t'canal bank and threw sods at 'im. A secret do, like. There were a big fuss about it. But they never found out who it were.' On this same canal, he saved a young woman from drowning and was awarded a Royal Humane Society certificate, for which George made a carved frame. It always hung on our wall in Mytholmroyd and Hebden Bridge, and now hangs in our London house.

'I were never one for getting on wi' t' regime. I always wanted it different. I remember at Robertshaw's I had to pack these cops into a basket. [Cops were long, thin bobbins of the spun cotton yarn, ready to be slotted into the looms' shuttles for weaving.] I wasn't so big, and I had to hold on to the side of the skep to stop myssen falling in when I put t'cops in wi' my other hand. One day I felt a hand on me shoulder, and there he were, old man Robertshaw. He said "Barker, we pay thee to use *two* hands." Aye, *two* hands. I've never forgotten that.

'I liked at Radcliffe's, no question o' that. But there were no money in it. And the man over me, he were only three year older nor me. So *he* weren't going to leave.

'Tom Stoney was manager at Radcliffe's. He were what I call a good boss. During th'unemployment, he had buyers down from Scotland. He showed 'em round and got lots of orders, big orders. They didn't want blankets wi' pile on 'em in Scotland. They said it's just fluff under t'bed. And it's only riven out o' t'cloth anyway, you know.

'When we set up in t'fish shop, Tom said to see how it did, and if it weren't right in a fortnight I could have me job back. He'd keep it open, like. People were on t'dole i' them days. I saw him i' t'Dusty [the Dusty Miller pub] and he said "How is it then?" and I said "All right." So he said "All right then." And that were that.

'Some time later I saw him again in t'Dusty, and he said "Have you got any money?" So I asked why. And he said "Well, if you have, put it in Universal Stores or Butlin's." I never did. But if I'd tekken his advice, I'd be worth a hundred thousand now, a hundred thousand.'

My father was always cautious with money, though he would always spend on things for my mother. Her 1930s beauty shines out in the earlier family snapshots. My father always looks equally dashing in his Fair Isle sweater. When they made their first £1,000 at the shop, he bought her a fox-fur stole. In wartime, when clothes were rationed, I remember she had it remade as a Russian-style fur hat. He put much of his savings into annuities, but they weren't inflation-proofed and were worth little when he retired.

'For the fish shop we borrowed £100 from my mother and £200 from Marion's mother. We soon paid it back. When my mother lent us £100, I didn't know she had 100 pence. She said, "Don't say nowt. But if the others get to know, they can have it as well, when it's paid back." But I never said, and they don't know yet.

'The fish shop were t'making of us. It were a good business in them days. By t'time war came we were taking £20 a week – which were a lot o'money then.' They had to let the shop go, when my father was conscripted into the National Fire Service and into munitions work. After the war, when their savings from that shop were running out, they decided to take on the corner shop in Hebden Bridge.

'On a Saturday night I remember my father [my grandfather Tom] would go down Mytholmroyd. They used to bring the papers out till eleven at night then, with racing results and such-like. T'butcher's would still be open. He'd have to get rid of his meat. There were no fridges then. At home we had a big fire oven, and my father would come back with a big piece o' meat and put it in. We'd be eating meat till Wednesday. Aye, it's true.

'The meat can't have been dear, because folk didn't have any money then – even my father, as a loom tackler, which were a good job in them days. He'd work Saturday afternoons, and any Sunday work that were going.'

After they'd put in a bid for the Hebden Bridge shop, the accounts showed it wasn't going as well as they'd been led to think. My mother said it would be best to pull out of the deal. But my father said he'd given his word, and they went ahead. To begin with, it wouldn't keep the two of them. Until they got a contract to sell newspapers, my mother served on in the shop, while he did a series of more or less dead-end jobs to make ends meet.

He was working as a petrol pump attendant when I was asked, at university, if I would answer questions for a social survey. The questions included 'father's occupation'. He would have been mortified. On my birth certificate he is 'master fish fryer'; on my wedding certificate, 'newsagent'. Small shops were then one accredited way out of the factory and into a kind of freedom. But it was hard to find a taker for the corner shop when he wanted to retire. Better mill wages, weekends off and longer holidays made most people think that the extra responsibility wasn't worth it.

The Hebden Bridge shop was like something out of another world, even then, when we moved in. It was still lit by gas – I remember the hissing sound of the mantles – and the lavatory was around the street corner. Much of the business seemed to be 'on tick' – that is, offering customers credit, which they often defaulted on. My parents stopped this, arguing that it only led to disputes.

For my mother, the Hebden Bridge business gave her the chance to get back to shop work, which she loved. For me, the great bonus was that the brother of the previous owner had accumulated a display cabinet of books – theoretically for sale, but really as his own library. Of an evening, I would go through from our house into the shop, pull back the glass doors, and take out a book to read. Many of them were by naturalists, but there were also Osbert Sitwell's memoirs and an early edition of *Animal Farm*. One day the books all disappeared, apart from *Animal Farm* and a small dictionary. These were held back for me and I still have them. Selling the books was probably part of the same hunt for funds which made my father sell almost all his rugby medals for the gold in them.

He had been a very good Rugby League winger, in a local amateur team. One ear was partly crushed, from the scrums. During the war, a local sport called billets was revived. My father took part. You balanced a cigar-shaped piece of wood (the billet) on a special stick, tossed it up, then hit it as far as you could. I went up to the fields to watch. Later I would sometimes go to rugby matches with him in Halifax. Sometimes, also, the dog track. I listened with him to the radio coverage of boxing matches. His guide to the likely winner was 'A good big 'un will always beat a good little 'un' and 'They never come back.'

My sister Elaine and I loved it when we went up to Heptonstall to have tea with one of his friends from his younger days. Apart from playing Whot and Lexicon card games, the big attraction was that we could encourage the two of them to sit and swap tales of 'the old days' – from their childhood and their own parents' days. The battles between different villages always featured: Royders versus Briggers and Briggers versus Heptonstallers.

This wasn't just a mild pastime. Sally's grandfather, Will Ashworth, walked to Heptonstall regularly, up the steep lane called the Buttress. He was courting a young Heptonstall woman, who became Sally's grand-mother. On his way back down he was always at risk, he said, of being followed and kicked with clogs. Heptonstall was already noted for its oddness. Sally's grandmother came from a large, unruly family; the father was often drunk. When the family went down to Hebden Bridge to have a group studio photo taken, the mother was shown suckling her latest baby.

The baby – one of eighteen – was Sally's grandmother, who did everything she could to put the childhood poverty behind her. She was very bright and had briefly been to the old, small, charity-funded Heptonstall grammar school, before the council-funded version opened in Hebden Bridge. In the sewing shops, on piece rates, she was famous for the work she got through. Much later, when I knew her, she was an ardent reader of the City page of the *Daily Mail*, and followed the advice on investments. 'Some people like spending. I like to save,' she said. She was generous with her money and a devotee of *The Archers*, *Coronation Street* and television football.

---

IN MY MOTHER'S WORDS:

'My father had a shuttle shop [a small factory] on Hangingroyd, down Hebden Bridge. He'd been working for someone else in Rochdale, but they came where the work was, in those days, and he came to Hebden. The shop was in my father's name, but they were partners. We moved to the house next to it when I was about twelve months old.

'Father died in 1919, in his fifties, in the flu epidemic, the house was a bit big. My mother took in lodgers, then looked round for something smaller. She kept on at Willie Redman for this house at Windsor View [a 'bottom' house, overlooking the Redman mill and just along from the Redman-run Methodist chapel]. They were Redman's houses, and Redman's agreed. There was only one bedroom and the people in it had a baby. It had to be a swap. We crossed at the bridge over the river. They were with a horse and cart with everything on, going one way, and we were going the other.'

My mother had a brother, Tom, and an older sister, Ethel. From the sewing shops, Ethel escaped to Kendal, where she eventually owned two shoe shops on the high street. I would go there during the summer holidays, sometimes with Elaine, sometimes alone. One of the places I loved was Kendal's big Carnegie Library. Ethel would drive us off for trips to Morecambe, a genteel resort we thought a lot less exciting than Blackpool. A pre-war Brownie snapshot shows Ethel, in her leather helmet, on a motorbike.

Tom worked in Rochdale but then served in the First World War. He came back with a wounded wrist, on which he wore a leather support for the rest of his life. He returned to work in Rochdale. When jobs in the Lancashire cotton trade collapsed, he switched to Thornber's hatcheries in Mytholmroyd. He remained always deeply loyal to the firm. Not surprisingly, he and my more anti-boss father did not get on.

'When my father died, our Ethel was already at Redman's, sewing,' my mother said. 'My mother also took a job there. She was a hand-sewer, sewing by hand. When I left school, they started me at Redman's. I don't think they dare do anything else, after the way my mother had gone on at Willie Redman about the house.'

When she went into Redman's, 'I was No. 114, I think it was. And I wouldn't be the last. There'd be some after me. And that was just the women sewing, not cutters or packers [both of which were men's jobs]. You had to put that number somewhere on all your work. You clocked in with that number as well.

'A lot of the housing then belonged to firms or to the Co-op. Broughton Street [near Windsor View] was built by Brown's, of Moss Lanes. They were back-to-back but with indoor lavatories – the latest thing. Unity Street [where I played Kick-Can] was partly Co-op, partly 'tinning shop' [a small metal-bashing firm in the old 'Tin Tabernacle' which had housed the Redman's chapel until a proper place, with its turrets, was built]. The houses could be hard to get. With the Redman's houses, you had to work there, to get in, even though they didn't out you out if you then left.

'One of the big cotton firms was Hoyle's [at Acre mill, in Old Town]. My uncle Fred Greenwood was one of Joshua Hoyle's bastards, so my mother always said. Fred got to be the boss at Acre mill [much later the site of a major asbestos scandal]. He had a big portrait of Joshua Hoyle in the house. My mother would say "Look at that!" Fred married my father's sister.' A Conservative candidate, who failed to win the local parliamentary seat after the Belcher scandal, was married to a Hoyle. It didn't help him.

'Uncle Fred's mother was wife to the gardener at Burnside, where Hoyle lived. Whenever the gardener was out, Hoyle would go visiting. She had other children as well. But this one – Fred – looked just like the son of old Hoyle – because he was.

'People were brought into Hoyle's from Liverpool, just like they used to bring them from the workhouse. It was like they brought the Irish to Luddenden Foot. Those houses that they pulled down along the roadside at t'Foot: they were all Irish. I suppose there aren't many Irish in t'Foot now, though there are lots o' funny names.

'Fred lived a very fast life. He thought Acre mill would never come to an end. But it did. Hoyle's sold the mill to Dunlop. That was the beginning of the end. Dunlop's sold it to Cape Asbestos, and that was it. Uncle Fred wouldn't take a job with Dunlop's, because it weren't the same as being in a family firm. He decided he'd wait for Acre mill to change hands again. I think he did get a job later, but he ended up really poorly off. He had nothing.

'You know I say I have cousins in Australia. Edith Habergam, she was Fred Greenwood's daughter. Habergams had a big shop on Market Street. During the First World War, those that tried to cause bother used to ask if it were a German name. There was a lot of that. Dehner's pork butchers on Bridge Gate had to close down because o' t'trouble. Dehner were a nice old man. Fred Dean was his son; he changed his name, but the father wouldn't. Russell Dean, who has the carpet shop at Mytholmroyd, is the grandson.

'On Sunday night it was the monkey run, between about half past seven and half past nine. You'd go to chapel to get out of the house, and you wouldn't come back. It were no use sitting in till half past seven, and then saying you thought you'd go out. It were too late then. "What do you want to go out at half past seven for?" On Saturdays, it was Market Street, between the first house and second house of the pictures.' The monkey run was similar to the Mediterranean evening *pasada*.

'We had right good times on the turnpike [the main road through Hebden Bridge to Mytholmroyd]. As traffic, there was only the trams. In the middle of those times, it was crowded like a football match losing [*losing* means 'coming out']. People came from all over, even down from Blackshaw Head. It was young people from about sixteen to twenty. After that they began to think it was a bit kiddish, and they'd go further afield for their entertainment, Halifax or Huddersfield.' My father bought a Yorkshire-made Scott motorbike and took my mother off on rides to nearby towns like Skipton or Burnley.

At about this time, Sally's mother, Marion, used to go on the monkey run with her good friend Edith, 'who always dressed in the most fashionable clothes,' she said. At the bridge which marked the Mytholmroyd end of the monkey run, 'there was always a group of lads,' she would say, 'and they especially made fun of Edith'. It was only by chance – too complicated a story to go into – that she realised, too late, that her daughter's new boy friend was the son of the noisiest of the lads at the bridge.

'The tram used to take an hour to cover the 7 miles to Halifax,' my mother said. 'Better transport came in then. When the bus and car traffic started, the job finished. The police prosecuted a few for 'loitering'. But they were only groups of girls.

'I met your dad at a dance at the old Band Hall, where the children's playground is on the park. I only got there, at fifteen and a half, because my mother and Ethel had to go out. I said "Mabel Horsfall's going to the Band Hall and I thought of going." I was told I could.' The Ashworths (Hebden Bridge) weren't keen on Donald Barker (Mytholmroyd), who was seven years older than her. The match stuck, but the wedding didn't take place until my mother was twenty-one.

'The Band Hall were pulled down later, but the Trades Club was built and had dances. I wasn't allowed to go to it, for some reason. They'd say, "And it's *Labour*, as well." Of course, that was the up-and-coming party in them days. The two main unions were the Garment Workers and the Dyers & Finishers.

'At Redman's, the Whitakers and a few other women were in charge. They ran Redman's, in their way. Frank Redman and the other bosses would always have a word to say to them. They were kind of teacher's pets, but they were very nice. They were all good workers. Sally's grand-mother, old Mrs Ashworth, was the figure above them, for work. You could tell the time by Mrs Ashworth running down to Redman's in her clogs. They all wore clogs in them days.'

It was a good marriage. When my father was in Leeds hospital, waiting for an aorta operation, he told my sister, 'Don't get upset if I don't make it. I've had a happy life.' This brutal stoicism was very 'Hebden'. When he died suddenly at home, some years later, the minister from the chapel called. I was sitting with my mother. She told him: 'When he went, I said "Come back, Donald, come back."' The minister, a young man, didn't know what to say. There was a long silence.

# 22. DOG

But for Louis Pasteur, I wouldn't be here to write this. On Saturday 26 May 1888, Tom Barker, my grandfather, then aged fourteen, was playing football with his friends in the middle of the turnpike road through Mytholmroyd when he was attacked by a mad dog. He tried to fight it off, but it bit him on his foot, hand and belly.

No one knew who owned this black and tan smooth-haired dog. It began its attacks at a farm called Paradise, where it worried a pup. It then roamed around Mytholmroyd, attacking or threatening various people, until a local man with a shotgun managed to kill it. A second boy, Frank Oldfield, was the only other person bitten. The *Hebden Bridge Times* looked on the bright side: 'if the dog had made its way to Hebden Bridge . . . , it would probably have played sad havoc among the excursionists from Oldham, hundreds of whom were then in the road, having just arrived [at the rail station] for Hardcastle Crags.'

Pasteur had administered his first anti-rabies vaccine in July 1885. Fortunately, word had already reached the West Riding. A local vet carried out a post mortem on the dog the next day, and confirmed that it had rabies. The carcase was burned. The local doctor who had given the boys first aid, and cauterised their wounds, sent a telegram to Dr Hime, the medical officer of health at Bradford, 'who has seen much of Dr Pasteur's method of inoculation, and for some time past has taken great interest in matters relating to hydrophobia' (as reported in the *Halifax Courier*). Dr Hime said that Tom and Frank should go to the Pasteur Institute in Paris as fast as possible.

The parents consented to this. But it would cost £25 for the journey to Paris and the twelve-day stay needed to complete the treatment. The

Barker and Oldfield parents said they could cover half of this. The *Halifax Courier* reported that the rest 'was most generously and quickly' given by neighbours and friends. Young Tom's fellow-workers at Robertshaw's mill also had a whip round. This was, so far as I can see, a classic story of working class self-help and mutual aid. If, for example, boss Robertshaw had chipped in, I'm sure it would have been reported in the press. On the Wednesday morning the two boys left by train with a junior doctor from the local practice. Going via London, Newhaven and Dieppe, they reached Paris by 10 am on Thursday 31 May and went off to their hotel. The first telegram confirming arrival was sent from Paris at 6.16 pm and reached Mytholmroyd at 7.15.

That same evening, the boys went to Pasteur's institute for him to give them their first injection. In the end, they had to stay fifteen days altogether, to give time for all the follow-ups. The doctor accompanying them wrote letters to the *Hebden Bridge Times* with microscopic clinical details of the treatment. In between the daily 11 am injections, the boys and, I presume, the junior doctor 'spent their time rambling through the thoroughfares of the gay city, and enjoying the sights there to be witnessed' (this is the *Hebden Bridge Times* at its most pompous). They would have had to ramble, or catch a bus: there was no Metro yet. A long extract from one Paris letter dated Tuesday 5 June was published in the *Times*' edition of Friday 8 June. It's wrong to think that everything in the past was slower than it is today.

Tom and Frank came back cured. A further £8 was collected locally to pay for the longer than expected stay. And the two boys got on with the rest of their lives.

I remember my grandfather with affection. He kept two beautiful red setters, Sheila and Paddy. He had the hen pen by the canal. On an allotment he had racing pigeons and other fancy varieties. Tumblers were the strangest breed. In mid-air they did what their name says they'd do. I could never understand how they got anywhere. After my grandmother Libby died young, I'm told that my grandfather took me on so many walks through the woods for company. In Redacre wood, red squirrels scuttered through the trees. In the fields above, I learnt about the most likely places to find edible mushrooms: 'where a mare has staled' [urinated]. By sharp experience I learnt the difference between stinging nettle and dead nettle.

There were five Barker brothers and one daughter, Marjorie, the youngest of them. As a girl, Marjorie was always a star at the Mytholmroyd 'demonstration' parade, with her Pierrette or Hawaiian costumes. She was my favourite aunt (though closely rivalled by Ethel). I remember her as always light-hearted and, into her nineties, always interested in what was going on. She has lived all her life, in Mytholmroyd, within a quarter of a mile, at most, of the house where she was born. When, as a child, I went over to visit her, she was living in a back-to-back with my widowed grandfather and my uncle Harry. Her husband, my uncle Leslie, was away in the forces. As Leslie's surname was Steward, the army, with its own unfathomable logic, assumed this was a version of 'Stuart' (which it wasn't). He was allocated to the King's Own Scottish Borderers, as almost the only Sassenach. He always remained fond of Scotland.

Marjorie's house was just along the street from where young Teddy Hughes, as she always called him, grew up. But by the time I used to look in at Marjorie's, the future laureate had moved house. In any event, in childhood, the five-year age gap was too great for either of us to be interested in the other.

Marjorie's house had various oddities which I liked. The bath, for example, was somehow slotted in under a fixed table in the kitchen. The rug in front of the open fire in the living room was a cosy cover for the little insects called silverfish (another name is springtail). My mother, who detested short forms of names, chose 'Paul' for me and 'Elaine' for my sister because she had a theory that they couldn't be abbreviated. To her, my father was always 'Donald', even though, to most other people, he was 'Donnie'. In my case, Marjorie got round this veto by calling me 'PB'.

The house was always welcoming and hospitable. But what I chiefly loved were the books and the gramophone. I knew no other house which had either of these.

The most tempting books were the bound volumes of Arthur Mee's *Children's Encyclopaedia*, with its attractive combination of text and pictures. First published as a fortnightly magazine, Mee's encyclopaedia was then sold from door to door in bound volumes. The text wove together stories and facts. Or, with the benefit of hindsight, I should perhaps say 'facts'.

Mee believed – like Montesquieu – that climate and environment had an overwhelming impact on human lives. The encyclopaedia had a page of comparative photographs. I remember one pairing which put a high-cheekboned, rather puritanical-looking, white Bostonian next to a serious-looking, rather handsome Red Indian. This was to demonstrate that a similar setting might produce a similar outcome. I don't remember any similar pairing of an Afrikaner and a Zulu.

You could say that this was a sort of photo-sociology. But it came close to the pseudo-science of craniology. Even in his own day, you could say that Mee was already a bit behind the times with such comparisons.

On the other hand, Mee was ahead of his time in including a well-illustrated item on how all the continents might once have been joined together as a single mass. The theory of continental drift was put forward in 1912 by Alfred Wegener, a German scientist. Wegener was convinced of it by the cross-continental parallels in flora and fauna and the matching coastal outlines. His idea was widely derided by other scientists, largely because Wegener was a meteorologist not a geologist, and he couldn't suggest any mechanism by which this shift could have been brought about. The theory of tectonic plates was only developed in the 1950s and 1960s, a quarter of a century after Wegener's death on an Arctic expedition. He had been right. This was an early lesson in never rushing to judgment over seemingly outlandish ideas.

The gramophone at Marjorie's house was under the lid of a veneered cabinet. The turntable ran by clockwork, which you wound up with a handle at the side. The records were 75 rpm shellac discs, kept in brown paper sleeves, with a cut-out circle in one side so that you could read the information on the disc. To play a record this way was an exciting ritual. There was 'The Laughing Policeman', which was highlighted by peals of laughter. It reminded me of the laughing clown robot at the entrance to the Fun House on Blackpool's Pleasure Beach. There were the famous monologues of Stanley Holloway, such as 'Sam, Sam, Pick Oop Thy Musket' and 'Albert and the Lion'.

This was many years before Holloway was cast as Mr Doolittle in the musical, *My Fair Lady*. He was London-born, but because of those monologues I'd always thought of him as one of the special race of northern comics, who were cherished for their separateness from the south:

Frank Randall with his seaside-postcard humour; Old Mother Riley and her daughter (Arthur Lucan, in drag, with his wife, Kitty McShane); Norman Evans, the great pantomime dame, with his 'Over the Garden Wall' vaudeville act. We saw all these on stage in Blackpool, on our annual visits. We kept up with them, in between times, in the pages of the *Radio Fun* and *Film Fun* comics.

And then Marjorie also had the records of George Formby, playing his little ukulele. I didn't understand the double meanings. I just loved the bounciness of the music, the silliness of the songs and, come to that, the silliness of George's polite Lancastrian voice. For our own children, years later, I bought Formby on LP.

My grandfather lived at Marjorie's house until his death. I was taken to see him when he was ill. I didn't realise he was on his death bed. There were no more walks with him up Redacre wood.

Aside from the dogs, he always had an all-black cat, and the cat was always called Tishy. It is a good, cattish name. But originally it was the name of a racehorse which was widely tipped to win the 1921 Cesarewitch at Newmarket. It came last. Tom Webster, the *Daily Mail*'s sports cartoonist, was a star in his own right, in a way unthinkable for any cartoonist today. He picked up on Tishy as one of his regular gallery of caricatures: a symbol of failure.

Tishy often changed her stride as she ran. Webster portrayed her as permanently cross-legged. He even drew a silent cartoon short, simply called *Tishy*. The audience needed no further explanation. The film was perhaps meant as a pilot for a series like Mickey Mouse or Felix the Cat, but it remained a one-off.

Our own cats have usually been all-black. We call them Tishy.

# 23. SCHOOL

I realise, in retrospect, what a difference a head teacher can make to a school. My own primary school, at Mytholmroyd, was very adventurous. The head had a display hive of bees in the room where we met for the daily assembly. Through the glass-sided walls, you could see them crawling over the combs while you sang the morning hymn. Extraordinarily, the school put on a performance of Maeterlinck's symbolist fairytale *The Blue Bird* (1908) in the local church hall. It is about a girl called Mytyl, her brother Tyltyl and their quest for happiness. I played a dream-child who brought Mytyl a bag – an old sugar bag, I recall – which held the 'gift' of childhood diseases: scarlet fever, measles and whooping cough. More of a poisoned chalice than a gift. To my chagrin, I had to kiss a girl called Kathleen, who played Mytyl. In his report to the governors, in the school log book, the head, Mr Eldridge, stated that the evening performances had been well attended, the Saturday matinee less so.

When I was doing the final checks on this book, I asked the British Library for a copy of *The Blue Bird*, to make sure I'd got the plot right. From their reserve store in Boston Spa, between Leeds and York, they brought down to London an English-language edition dated 1917. From an old rubber stamp, I saw that the book had originally been in the library of the Leeds teacher training college (where my mother- and father-in-law both studied). I ran my eye down the list of characters. Several names had been pencilled in as possible players: a Boocock, a Watson, but also, very clearly written, 'P. Barker'. The school must have borrowed this play-text from the college. Maybe it was even the prompt copy.

At Hebden Bridge grammar school, the head was Herbert Howarth. He grew up in a family who farmed on the outskirts of Halifax. He was a long-standing Labour Party supporter. He never promoted party politics at school. But he did strongly support the idea of merging the grammar school into an early comprehensive. Labour Party grandees tended to turn up at speech day to give the prizes. The principal school song was the German student anthem, '*Gaudeamus Igitur*'.

The school didn't teach German, but Howarth thought it was intellectually essential. He gave me his black-letter German–English, English–German dictionary (1888 edition). I only ever used it, years later, when I tried, without success, to teach myself the language. He also seemed to think I needed a glimpse of a non-Hebden world and lent me a translation of Balzac's scatological *Contes drolatiques*. I read them, but I don't remember giving the book back to him. It just disappeared. I suspect that my parents returned it to him without saying anything.

To Herbert Howarth's adventurousness, I owe the first production of Shakespeare – and the first professional theatrical performance, outside pantomime and music hall – that I'd ever seen. I was in Form Three, I think, when we trooped across to the Co-op Hall in Hebden Bridge to see an extraordinary version of *Macbeth*. I was riveted by the swirling, bright costumes, the wonderful lighting, the high melodrama. It was all carried out by six or seven women who took every part, played the music, changed the scenes. They called themselves the Osiris Players. One day they were there, with much of their gear piled into an old Rolls-Royce. Next day they were gone.

I never forgot the name. But who were the Osiris Players? Where had they come from? From time to time, over the years, I asked people about them. The name meant nothing, and was in no reference book. I came to assume that they were a group that had acted together for two or three years, and then disbanded. It wasn't till 1994, thanks to a chance discovery at the Theatre Museum in London, that I found that the Osiris Players were the country's first-ever all-women theatre group. They toured Shakespeare (mostly) and other plays, for more than thirty years, under the benevolent dictatorship of an amazing woman called Nancy Hewins. In gratitude for that day at the Co-op Hall, I found out as much as I could – including talking to some former Osiris actresses – and wrote the group up. This was something no one had ever done before. Afterwards, I was delighted to be asked to contribute a Hewins entry for the *Oxford Dictionary of National Biography*. At last, the Osiris Players were getting some of their public due.

At school, Herbert Howarth took what were called 'general studies' lessons himself. During them, he specialised in gnomic bursts of wisdom, like 'Never run after a bus, a woman or an idea; there'll be another one along in a minute.' He struck most of his young listeners as very boastful about his contacts and his achievements. It was only when I was much older that I realised he was telling the truth. The problem lay with our own insularity, which presumably he was trying to shake up.

His nickname was 'C.I.'. No pupil ever called him anything else (except to his face). It was not clear what the initials stood for. The most likely explanation was Criminal Investigator (modelled on CID). In my day he did very little caning. Gradually it was overtaken by writing lines: at home to begin with, then in after-school detentions. I had much experience of these, being punished as unstoppably fond of 'talking in class'.

The head with the highest reputation in present-day Hebden is Tony Greenwood. Two days after I talk to him, he will be fifty-six. The day after that, he'll be celebrating twenty-six years as headmaster of Colden school. His intake of 106 children is always over-subscribed. Here on the rainy hilltop, the families he teaches have gone from being almost all in agriculture to practically none. 'We have,' he says, 'one child from a working farm.'

He is a head of the same energising kind as Eldridge and Howarth. You can tell how good a school is the moment you walk in. There's something in the air, like an orchard smelling of apple or pear blossom. And this is true of Colden. All the rooms have little cardboard labels in Spanish. 'It's an up-and-coming language. I'm a frequent walker in Spain. It does no harm.' As he says this, we are looking out of the window of his room, at the back of the school. We see fields leading up to moorland. The farms, or what used to be farms, have evocative, eccentric names, like Egypt or Scotland. (William Barker, the pioneer of ready-made fustian, was born at Scotland.) Greenwood is obviously the guiding spirit of the school, with his quick brown eyes and the brightest of bright ties.

The change in the local social mix in recent years, he thinks, is 'all to do with altitude'. The higher-up a house is, the more expensive it is. 'Up here, if you had the money, you can buy quite big detached stone houses. One man is a judge, a recorder. Another is a senior solicitor.' He points out of the window. 'That one used to be a dentist. This one runs his own public relations business. Over there used to be one of the higher-ranking Catholic priests in the army. In among, there's quite a little group of home-workers. There are a few chickens and goats and so on, but that's mostly it for farming.' One big house, with land, has been put up for sale at a million pounds.

Colden pupils are taught at traditional desks. 'They came with me. I bought them at 50p each. It's better for children than sitting all round a table. It gives each child a private space. And prospective parents also like them.' But there is no school uniform and no Latin motto. Some of the parents come long distances to bring their children to Colden, passing several other primary schools on the route of their car. Calderdale borough doesn't operate a catchment area. Between 60 and 70 per cent of the Colden children go on to Calder High School. Many of the rest go to two selective Halifax schools which still have an eleven-plus exam. A few others go off to public schools.

Tony Greenwood now lives a few miles away from Colden school, but he has strong local roots. His grandfather was a violin-maker, who lived above Hardcastle Crags, along the road to Greenwood Lee and Higher Greenwood – where all the Greenwoods in the world originate from. As a child, he used to walk down into the Crags.

He regularly takes the top class on a walk of 6 or 7 miles around the hillside. It is a lesson in local history. They look for traces of the Civil War. They find out what 'mullions' and 'lintels' are. At one time, Tony Greenwood tells me, he had a regular dream of 'being in a derelict ghost town, with broken windows and people peering out. Eventually I realised it must be Heptonstall, as I first saw it.'

He is ironic about the political correctness of the people down in the Hebden valley bottom. 'The mad ideas of Hebden Bridge. . . . It gets a bit better once you get up to Heptonstall.' The higher-up you live, the more rational, he suggests, and grins. He tells me a story of Riverside primary school – in the buildings of the old Hebden Bridge grammar school – which suffered an outbreak of nits (that is, lice eggs on the hairs of the head). The head launched a campaign to kill the lice off. He then received an angry letter from one parent: 'Even lice have a right to live.'

Greenwood worked in a cotton mill as a holiday job. He hated it – 'The boredom, and you felt you were feeding the devil.' Greenwood's mother worked in the same mill, on the looms, 'but finally as a welfare worker, which she loved'. His passionate detestation of mill work reminds me of Lady Willie, and his hatred of working at the looms in Jack Bridge mill. In the chill and rain, I can still feel an emptiness where this Colden mill used to be.

Kindness and calm radiate from Tony Greenwood, like a portrait in a church shop. He is fascinated by the Colden surroundings, even after a quarter-century in this job. 'Colden is Colditz', they used to say. He is intensely proud of the school. It's built on the 'long house' principle: no corridors, and each room opening into the next. He's hoping to get some refurbishment money. But, fortunately, 'all these 1870s board schools were very well built'.

This is the last day of term. He is about to go off to lie on a Greek beach. He'll then walk the Santiago de Compostela pilgrim way from Moissac, in south-west France, to the Pyrenees. He's already done the Spanish end of the walk. It makes about as fierce a change from Colden as you could think of. But he remains as attached as anyone I've met to the idea of Hebden (and its environs) as a place.

He's especially proud of his name. 'There are more Greenwoods in Hebden Bridge, proportionately, than anywhere else in the world.' When I check the local phone book, it has three columns of Greenwoods. Many are not in Hebden Bridge itself. Nowadays so many users are ex-directory, or only talk on mobile phones, that it's hard to tell what the real total is. On the wall of the town hall's newly named Greenwood Room, the council has hung a mid-nineteenth-century oil painting of Hebden Bridge, which shows it at the very beginnings of its industrial take-off. The rail line and the canal are here, two or three mill chimneys and a big, four-square chapel. That is about it.

I walk back down into Hebden from Colden school. I go through Heptonstall. The octagonal chapel is open, and I look in. A notice says it is 'the oldest Methodist church in the world in continuous use'. A very precise claim, somehow very Protestant, very Nonconformist. The chapel was founded in the 1740s. John Wesley preached at Heptonstall for the last time in 1786. In the calm, galleried interior a large clock faces the preacher, to keep him to time. Even eternity has to be measured out.

# 24. MARKET

Mrs Durancyk has a jewellery and pottery shop on Hope Street, named after the chapel, and across from where Hebden Bridge Co-op had its headquarters. Her window display of jewellery has nine-carat gold rings, set with topazes or emeralds. The gold bangles and chains are also nine-carat. A forty-four-piece silver-plate cutlery set is £500: a suitable wedding present. An 'SOS Talisman' can store 'information to identify the wearer and vital medical information'. A copper bangle has 'magnets for rheumatism'. The pottery window features 'collectables': floral ceramic bouquets, little dogs, dragons, also pewter tankards and flasks. Two statuettes portray young women in ceramic ball gowns: 'Olivia' is dressed in green, 'Fiona' in red.

The name on the shop door is 'T&G Durancyk', but Mrs Durancyk is now a widow. She looks tiny behind the glass counter and is very friendly. I remember her daughter from school, I say, 'partly because the name was so memorable'. 'Yes,' she says, 'not Greenwood or Sutcliffe,' and she smiles. The Durancyk story is an example of the earlier one-by-one migration into Hebden. Her Polish-born husband was in the British army – the Tank Corps, she tells me. 'He fought in Italy. Afterwards, they had the choice of going to America or staying in England. He was stationed at Catterick camp, in the North Riding. He came visiting Hebden Bridge with a friend. That's how I met him.'

Her business has been here for many years, 'in one set of premises or another'. I ask her if her children still live in Hebden Bridge. 'Oh, they're away now.' I ask where, thinking that they have perhaps moved to Leeds or even London. 'Mytholmroyd and Luddenden Foot', she says. A mile or three. . . .

The neighbouring shop is painted in black. It is a combined acupuncturist and hair stylist. The hair-cutting is done at dark-stained pinewood dressing tables, with large mirrors. It is all designed to look very smart and discreet: except that, from the street, you are very much on show. 'If you've got it, flaunt it,' as they say in Cheshire.

The public library is next along the street. It lies opposite a local police station which, amazingly, still functions. Vast amounts of money have been put into making the library's premises a bit flashier, much better for staff, more computer-friendly and such-like. But the place is desperately low on books. The core of the 'local interest' section is a file of press cuttings. It is easier to get information from the tourist office than from the library. The sight saddens me, thinking again of all that I owe to libraries.

At one table, a man, who looks to be in his sixties, is reading the *Yorkshire Post*. Another, younger man, who seems to be some sort of friend, comes into the library, walks across to him, and says grimly: 'Hope you're not reading that rag.' The *Yorkshire Post* is a Conservative newspaper, politically. The Hebden Bridge newsagent's now sells vast quantities of the *Guardian*. Unfortunately, this doesn't always breed tolerance.

'It's not much fun being retired, and having time but no money,' the older man says. 'You should have become a teacher,' his sort-of-friend says. 'Then you'd have had some money to retire on. It wouldn't be clogs to clogs in two generations.' With such friends, who needs enemies?

The Hebden Bridge Sports and Social Club is one place where the locals drink. So is the Pennine Club, which used to be known as the 'Con. Club' (despite the name, no one had to sign any Tory pledge). It's too early for either of these. I walk on towards Pennine Provisions. On this site Ted Hughes's father had his tobacconist's shop. All very modest. But Pennine Provisions is as fancy a grocer's as you could hope to find this side of Harrods. Cornish sea-salt. Japanese *wakame* (apparently a dried sea-vegetable). Whole goat's milk. Organic tomato juice. Home-made gooseberry jam. Cranberry *pressé*. Falafel mix. And, last but not least, Todmorden Pexommier: 'creamy Camembert-style cheese made entirely from Todmorden organic milk'.

Hope Baptist church is still here, opposite the picture house. Founded in 1857, it bears a plaque in memory of the Revd John Fawcett, 1740–1817, 'gifted scholar, devoted pastor and inspired preacher'. I have only once set foot inside these doors. I sat in the gallery to hear Isobel Baillie, one of the most famous British choral sopranos of her day, sing the female lead in Mendelssohn's *Elijah*. Until then, I'd never heard a music professional.

Enigma Ink, the local tattoo shop, is directly across from the Hebden Bridge masonic lodge. Hebden is a tattoo capital. The designs seem even more popular among the women than the men. Enigma Ink is the place to get another one added. (For laser deletions you have to go to Mytholmroyd.) There is a Chapel of Rest to one side of the tattooist's and the Calderdale Yogic Centre on the other. Jehovah's Witnesses once had their Kingdom Hall a few yards away, but that brand of salvation has withered. Behind Enigma Ink lies Word of Mouth, a crafts shop which offers courses in jewellery making, crochet, stencilling and quilt making. In the tattoo shop window is an image of Shiva. Inside, a man and a woman are stretched out, full-length on two separate beds.

The owner, Sarah Knowles, five years a tattooist, has been here for eighteen months. She has two assistants, and five people waiting to be apprenticed, she says. 'It can take between one year and three years. But some people are naturally able.' She herself is self-taught. She was an assistant manager at a Halifax tattooist's, before coming here.

'It's all custom-designed,' she says. 'People come in with an idea and we have a consultation. Older people stick to the older "flash" designs. Younger ones are going into Japanese. It's vanity, isn't it? Wanting to stand out from the normal, the ones without tattoos. We're finding a lot more women wanting big pieces, not just little ones. Customers ask for what they see on television. They want a tattoo to remember.

'I was a late bloomer. I had strict parents. I was twenty-two before I had my first tattoo. A little butterfly. Even now, there's a prejudice against tattoos, but in Hebden everyone's been lovely, very supportive. I've one girl who designs her own tattoos. I won't do logos or sports and football memorabilia. I try to discourage customers from using names in their tattoos. I ask them, "How long have you been together?"'

The sittings can be six hours at a time. 'The pain threshold changes day by day. It is quite painful. I like *having* tattoos – not having them *done*. But you get out of the pain.' She has a big cover-up tattoo on one arm, erasing a design she wants to forget. On her other arm she has Japanese-style imagery. She has a small tattoo on the side of her neck, and a stud in her lip. She is thirty-six years old.

This being Hebden, she offers inks that even vegans can use (so no cochineal red, from crushed beetles). She thinks Hebden is 'a beautiful place'. Even if it has 'a dark side to it', it is a lot better than Halifax, which 'has become a glorified row of pubs, with less and less shops'. Hebden Bridge reminds her of the Brontës' Haworth, 'I've never seen so many tourist shops as here. Hebden Bridge is like the little town that time forgot. It's always fifteen or twenty years after anywhere else. But it's a solid community. Everybody's different. It's amazing you can get this in a single village.'

Nearby, on a car park, the Hebden Bridge market takes place on two successive days each week. The Thursday market is like a cheaper version of Pennine Provisions: fancy cheeses, fresh vegetables – but with added meat. The customers at the stalls are what you would expect: middle class, tending towards bohemian. But the Wednesday market is for second-hand goods. The Wednesday trade is a sharp social contrast with Thursday's.

On Wednesdays, Rod has what he calls an 'antiquey' stall. He also has a shop in Mytholmroyd. Looking round, he says, 'There's cheap and there's cheap. I don't think this is a very wealthy town – though there *are* wealthy people.' A few yards away, some very un-wealthy young women are studying an array of children's second-hand clothes. One stall-holder is packing up. She says, 'It's the recession, isn't it? I'm downsizing and selling what I don't want.' On Wednesdays, it seems that anyone can set up a stall.

Among the other ways of looking at it, Hebden is a tale of two markets.

# 25. STORY TIME

TELLING A TALE (1970S):

## WARTIME

The Ministry of Food inspector looks in at a Hebden Bridge butcher's.

'I believe there's a lot of dealing going on in black market meat. Have you heard anything about that, Rex?'

'Nay. That's news to me. Can't help you there, lad.'

So off the inspector goes. And when he seems well out of the way, the butcher goes on his usual trip, driving his van up through Crow Nest wood to the hamlet of Wood Top. He calls on his old friend, the farmer.

'Owt for me today?'

'Oh aye. Wait in t'kitchen. Wife'll be down in a minute. She's having a lie-in.'

The butcher waits. The wife comes down for a chat over a cup of tea. The farmer comes in from the barn with the gutted carcass of a pig.

At just that moment, the butcher glances out of the window. To his horror, he sees the food inspector coming up the lane through the fields.

'Get thee back into bed, lass,' the farmer tells his wife. Which she does, and snuggles down well, up to her chin. They wrap the pig in a blanket and put it into the bed, under the coverlet, alongside her.

The inspector reaches the farmhouse, knocks on the door and the farmer lets him in.

'Na then. What can I do for thee this morning?'

'Just looking in to say hello and to see papers.'

He begins with a cup of tea, chatting to the farmer and his butcher friend. He finishes looking at the food rationing forms. But then:

'How's the wife? I see she's not here.'

'Oh, she's been right poorly. She's still in bed, like.'

'Well, I'd better wish her well, before I go.'

He opens the staircase door and goes on up. He looks in at the bedroom.

'How're you getting on, Ada? I'm told you're not well.'

'Thanks for asking. It's very kind of you. I weren't at all well. But now I'm mending champion.'

The food inspector goes happily along his way. And the butcher comes back that night to collect the pig.

'I remember a Ministry of Food official saying to me: "If they're short of what to eat in Hebden, it's their own fault. They shouldn't be."'

— Albert Cockcroft, sewing shop cutter

## THE NAVVIES AT DAWSON CITY

There was one woman at Heptonstall, who was making money while her husband was out – being a prostitute for the navvies from Widdop reservoir.

One day, someone tells him that he ought to go back home, to see what's going on. So he goes back, in the middle of the day. And there she is, at it.

But she was a big woman. She just got up and threw him out, saying he should mind his own business.

He was back a week later, knocking at the door and shouting, 'Hey, lass, let me in, and a won't believe me own eyes no more.'

— Alice Ashworth, grandmother-in-law

## HEPTONSTALL FUN

There were one girl that used to dry her hair by putting it in the mangle. It were an old wood-roller cast-iron mangle. She had long black hair. One day the mangle clocked [broke down], and they couldn't get her hair out. They had to call somebody to it.

He was the local undertaker. As he walked out from the house, everyone was dumbstruck. Where was the body?

Afterwards, we laughed and laughed.

— Cross Inn landlord

## A CHARACTER

Talby was a right character. He was going back home up the Buttress to Heptonstall, after a bowls match. His bag came undone and the bowls fell out and ran down hill.

'We've nobbut to find t'jack,' he said. 'T'others'll be ligging [lying] next to it.' He meant he were that fine a bowler.

— Clifford Wright, fustian presser

## ANOTHER

The vicar of Heptonstall got up into t'pulpit and said that, as his subject for the day, he'd take the story of the widow's mite.

Dick Pitts, who were t'verger, leans across to me and whispers, 'What's he on about? *Might?* We know they all *will* — except for that ginger-haired un down there at t'front.'

— Clifford Wright

# GREENWOODS' BY-NAMES

With so many Greenwoods in Hebden, by-names were the only way to tell families apart. A by-name could last down the generations. 'Jimmy Spicy' or 'Harry Swop,' to begin with, but then, for example, 'She were a Dauber, you know, before she married a Sutcliffe.' Such by-names were seen as a Hebden trademark. This box combines lists kept by Jessie Gill, of Machpelah, Hebden Bridge, and Stanley Greenwood, of White Hole farm, Crimsworth.

Spicy (sweet stall)
Dauber (painter)
Putty (plumber)
Cabby (hansom driver)
Muck-cart (night-soil man)
Booty (boot and shoe shop)
Chips (fish and chip shop)
Swop (railwayman; allegedly
    said 'All swap,' not 'All
    change,' at station)
Tom o'Jacks o'Sally
    (grandmother's names)
Israel (grandfather's name)
Lewis (ditto)
Dick o'Nancy's
    (grandmother's name)
Teddy Kitty (ditto)
o'Jonty (son of Jonathan)

Jack o't'Den (house name)
Jack o't'Lea (ditto)
Babby House Hill (ditto)
Jooar at Thurrish (Joseph;
    ditto)
Jooanie at White Hoyle
    (Jonas; ditto)
'Nomic (lived at the
    'Economic' cut-price
    store)
Bloaters (favourite food)
Porridge (ditto)
Ping Pong (favourite game)
Chinny
Long Frank
Little Tom
Red Leonard
Swank

## WEAVERS

A man stops next to me outside the Co-op weaving shed in its latter days. We look in together at the clatter and dust of the looms.

'Torture chambers, them places. I've been off sick since February, and I'm in no hurry to get back. I used to be in shop work, now I'm in engineering, a tackler. I must try to get back to shop work, but it's nice weather for playing.

'I don't mind working, but I won't be *rushed*. The boss came in and told me to hurry up. I told him where to get off. I said, "We're doing the work. You're just a passenger. We're not on piece rate here, just time rate. Don't come bothering me."'

## BUSINESS

'I wish people wouldn't come into Hebden Bridge. It brings no money into t'valley. We were happy as a backwater. Whether they're visiting or coming to live, they only ever come in the shop on Saturday or Sunday. We used to have twenty-seven electricians, and we were busy with twenty-seven electricians. Now we have three. There's no industry in the town now. Once there were eight mills within 150 yards of here. Now they're all shut or turned to other purposes.'

When this shop came up for sale, there were no takers. It was finally let in 2010.

– Geoff Lord, owner of electrical sales and repairs shop

## THE NEWCOMER

When I moved into Unity Street, the woman from the house opposite came across and explained that the hook on my wall was *her* hook and the hook on her wall was *my* hook. They were for putting up clothes lines on the Monday. We oughtn't to stretch them across first thing in the morning in case anyone further down the street had a car and needed to drive off to work. But after that, both sides of the street put their lines across, and no traffic could come through. That way, everybody knew where they were.

— Bookshop assistant

## SUTCLIFFES

I was in the post office when a man came through from the sorting office and threw an envelope on the counter. 'It just says, "Sutcliffe, Hebden Bridge". Can you do owt wi' that?' Laughter all round.

— Alice Longstaff, photographer

## ON THE RANT

Beer was cheap, and it were stronger then. There were no licensing laws. Talking about a neighbour, my mother would say 'He's off again, old James, on t'rant.' As they did in those days. Workers would knock off and go on a rant till a job was finished, if it seemed too difficult. Old Dan Crabtree, at Eastwood dye works, used to take the workers out on a rant with him. If you got into a pub, there might be somebody there, ranting. They'd be paying and you'd be all right for the day. For men, communal life was more or less pub life.

— Everitt King, secretary, Farmers' Association

# 26. SWITZERLAND

## EATING OUT

The Relish restaurant is at Oxford House, Albert Street. It calls itself a 'global eatery'. On the menu are Sri Lankan red curry, French onion and hazelnut tart, and Tuscan beans with aubergines. The restaurant says it won the Vegetarian Restaurant Award, 2008.

But why are its Victorian premises called Oxford House? In the late nineteenth century, Christian Socialists and Oxford-based extension lecturers took a special interest in Hebden Bridge. The locals seem to have preferred spiritual uplift to revolutionary upheaval. Hence, probably, the name.

One of the attractions for such well-intentioned visitors was Joseph Greenwood's worker cooperative mill at Nutclough. The mill even named its huge coal-fired boiler 'Tom Hughes' after the Ruskinite campaigner (and author of *Tom Brown's Schooldays*). The boiler was still blazing cheerfully away as I walked down past it, as a schoolboy, into Hebden Bridge

---

## THE ALLOTMENT

At an allotment next to Nutclough wood, a blonde woman in jeans is gardening with a big box of slug pellets beside her and how-to-garden guidebook in her hand.

---

## THE PHILANTHROPIST

Jason Elliott runs his plastics recycling firm from a small office in the former Hebble End mill. We meet in Hebden's hippiest café. The waitress addresses me as 'Love'. Not everything changes. Jason is thin-faced and balding; he wears a green T-shirt, jeans and trainers; he is energetic and, I'm sure, a very good salesman. He helps to finance Hebden arts and ecological events.

Like Polly Webber, he tries to do good by stealth. 'We never say "Save the planet".' Hebden has 'two different communities, about 50–50. But locals should feel they can speak up, even if they can't say "anti-disestablishmentarianism". The hopeful sign is that the under-thirties, on both sides, are less aware of the differences. They have no personal memories of life before the hippies.' After an itinerant life, partly as a photographer, he came to Hebden in 2005. He's now forty-five. He thinks he 'may spend ten years in Hebden Bridge', and then move on.

---

## BILLETS

After the old hilltop grammar school in Heptonstall closed, it was a branch of the Yorkshire Penny Bank from 1898 to 1954. At primary school, we were given a passbook and encouraged to put our pennies in. The penny bank is now the Yorkshire Bank, a subsidiary of the Clydesdale Bank; I still make use of it.

The wood on its old grammar school desks is as black as tar. The head teacher's own desk rises up like a pulpit. Now a local museum, a photograph shows 'Eric Barker' (a cousin of my father's) playing billets at Heptonstall in the 1960s. The last 'world championship' of billets was held near Halifax in 1970, a caption says. The winner hit his billet 'ten score and 20 yards'.

---

## HOLLINS

There are lots of places called 'Hollins'. The name means that it's a place where holly grows. This is a shrub well adapted to Hebden weather and, in the old days, able to survive Hebden pollution. I reach this particular Hollins by going over a little humpbacked bridge which crosses Foster brook. On the right is the Hebden Bridge cricket pitch, 'Salem Field', where two people are walking their dogs. I walk up the steep lane, paved with old packhorse stones, to the higgledy-piggledy hamlet.

It is a jumble of little old houses and criss-crossed steps – like Provence, without the sun. There are clusters of hollyhocks and even larger clusters of nettles. When I delivered mail here, as a temporary postman, Hollins was half-derelict. One tiny cottage was home to a notorious madwoman, who was best avoided. Several similar places in Hebden got demolished. I don't know how Hollins escaped. Out of sight, out of mind?

On the other side of Foster bridge, Redman's mill has been replaced by newly built houses and flats. Hollins itself has been spruced up like someone going to a wedding.

---

## CAUTIOUS DOES IT

The sign on the side of a van says: 'R.B. Blackburn: all aspects of joinery considered.'

---

## SOLIDARITY

A Palestinian flag will fly on the town hall for five days, as a tribute to a group of refugee children who are visiting Hebden.

———————

## DOG SHOWS

Kay Barret has a 1½-acre smallholding, called Greystones Barn, high up the Crimsworth valley. She bought it from the Savile estate. She breeds and shows deerhounds and writes about them in dog magazines. 'Shows are a good way to meet people.' She came to Hebden in 1975 and used to be a Calderdale borough councillor.

'The village was so beautiful, though not so much so now. Up here is still the most beautiful place. The winters can be bad. Last winter there was so much snow, the council ran out of grit. I ran out of water, it froze, and I had to boil snow. Fortunately the electricity still ran, but it was a hard time.' She writes fiction, though none of this has been published yet, and she paints. 'It's hard to make a living out of it.' Once, she says, Hebden Bridge was something of a mystery, 'but now, if I say "Hebden Bridge", people have always been there or know a friend who has.'

She goes back to feed her dogs, who are yelping for their meal.

———————

## THE ART GALLERY

David Wright shows me round the Paula Rego prints in the gallery at the top floor of Linden mill. He is grey-haired and mild-mannered. He grew up in Birmingham, where his father was a sculptor – often taking on municipal commissions, such as war memorials. He was at the Slade school in London with Rego and her future husband, Vic Willing. David used to run the arts department at college in Wakefield. He came to Hebden Bridge in 2003, because a student of his had recommended it.

He took a studio in the mill, and then had the idea for a gallery. I remember coming to one of David's first shows – also of Paula Rego. As I look round the new show, I say that her spiky pictures, like nursery tales gone mad, suit Hebden very well. I don't pursue the analogy.

Rego comes up sometimes. She goes off hunting in local junk shops for old clothes to put in her paintings.

---

## THE STATION

The Friends of Hebden Bridge Station keep a regular supply of fresh flowers in place. The station looks as polished up as if the crew for a period costume drama are about to arrive. The Victorian lettering is unchanged. Among the signs are 'Lamp Room' and 'Parcels Office'. Disabled children are sitting on the York-stone pavement outside, waiting for two minibuses to take them to Hardcastle Crags.

Without the railway, Hebden Bridge and Mytholmroyd would have been only dots on the map. The demolished coal sheds and warehouses have been replaced by car parks with space for 171 cars. There is a pleasant little coffee shop in the station building. The men in the ticket office are notably cheerful and helpful. The 'foot-fall' – that is the total of those leaving and arriving – was 627,045 in 2009–10, well up on the year before. On average, more than 1,700 a day. That's mainly due to commuters.

---

## PIGEONS

Charlie Roberts is watching a flock of his pigeons wheel around in the sky above one of his huts. The birds in the air are all hens, the cocks are inside: 'All grandchildren of champions. But we've got as many eggs as we want. So we've separated the sexes.'

Charlie is cheerful, stubby, slightly red-faced. His pigeons are homers. The sport attracts far fewer people than it did. 'The homing club in Hebden Bridge became so small that we merged with Todmorden.' He sends his racers over to Littleborough, in Lancashire, for example. Not all of them come back.

'I lost seven last week. It's peregrine falcons and sparrowhawks. They say that a sparrowhawk will kill three wild birds a day, and ten more if it has a nest. People blame farmers for the decline in wild birds. We hardly see any around here any more. But it isn't that, it's the raptors. They should be culled back to a reasonable number.'

---

## HORSES

In a field behind Mitchell mill, beside the lane up to the moor, I see five mares and four foals. The higher fields have even more horses – horses as a form of entertainment. This is the way up to Bogg Eggs farm – a wonderfully mysterious name (and home to one of the Hawden Hall murderers), but now rechristened 'Allswell Farm'. I hope the change is temporary. The farm calls itself an 'equestrian centre'. Between the farmhouse and a small square reservoir, which used to feed the mill, there are many more horses. It could be a scene in Wiltshire or Surrey – except that, up here, the landscape is much more unyielding.

The farmhouse is now dominated by two big sheds. No sign of anyone around, but two Jack Russells try to yap me away as I try to get nearer.

The moor beyond is dotted with bleak, isolated houses – one of them called Weather House – and a few functioning farms. It is not a picturesque place.

---

## BONSALL'S

I keep being told: 'If Bonsall's goes, that's it.' This is what's now called a hardware store and would once have been called an ironmonger's. It's at the edge of where the weekly market is set up. The shop has been there for ever, it almost seems. Certainly, for as long as I've known Hebden

Bridge. The Bonsall family no longer run it, but the new owners keep the name, because it evokes continuity and affection.

You can buy absolutely anything there for your DIY. The shelves are packed with an extraordinary miscellany of goods. To many people, both newcomers and long-time locals, Bonsall's embodies what's left of local shopping – which is not much – in among the smart new shops for the fancy trade, the organic stores for the ecologically correct, and the coffee and tea cafés for the tourists, who wander around on Saturdays and Sundays, trying to kill time. Most Hebden people go to the Todmorden or Halifax supermarkets for their main weekly shopping. They have the choice of Morrison's, Sainsbury's, Tesco, Aldi or Lidl.

Bonsall's seems busy enough, when I go in. But I have met several people who tell me they 'shop there just as much as possible, to keep it going'.

One thing in Hebden is highly traditional: shops and cafés nearly all close at five.

---

## CHARITY

In St George's Square, a gypsy girl – maybe from Romania – is squatting on the pavement, trying to sell *The Big Issue of the North*. A charity chugger for the Shelter housing charity walks briskly past her. They don't even glance at each other.

---

## A CENTENARY

Harold Crabtree's clothes and shoe shop celebrates 100 years in business by putting on show a bright white wedding dress made entirely from bio-degradable bags converted into textile. The dress stands alone in one window. The designer's name is given as Oliver Crabtree.

## JOKER

On a sunny Saturday morning, a middle-aged man with a bright-red Mohican haircut walks along the canal towpath. He has a large beer-belly and clerk-type glasses. His T-shirt says 'Son of Jackal'. Two young women are with him; one of them may be his daughter. He is telling them a string of lesbian jokes.

---

## INVESTORS

At the table next to me in the Squeeze coffee shop, a man and a woman are having a long discussion about English and French property laws. Which are better? And is it worth investing in Hebden Bridge?

---

## SWISS STYLE

David Fletcher, founder of Calder Civic Trust (1965) and Pennine Heritage (1979), says: 'When Herbert Howarth took us on a school trip from the grammar school to Switzerland in 1949, I thought to myself that I wanted Hebden Bridge to be like this – attractive, efficient, well-kept, a good environment. And it's worked. It's not just about conservation. Locally, there are conflicts and rows, of course. People come here and think they've found their own Nirvana. There's a lot of position-taking. But Hebden has always been changing.'

# 27. SISTERS

Mayroyd House, where I talked to Annie Whitaker and her sister May, was a curious square house, like a child's drawing. The canal was on one side. Beyond lay the dereliction of old mills. The Whitaker sisters and I all remember watching the largest mill burn down. They tell me that there were three mill fires altogether hereabouts. 'This was called Hellfire Corner.' And they both laughed.

The stairs went up through the middle of the house, lit by a long chapel-like window. There used to be four four-square rooms on each floor, with four-square attics and cellars. Now, in 1978, the sisters lived upstairs, in their late seventies, with their brother Frank, an electrician, downstairs. The Whitakers were cousins of my mother's. Annie and May said that, at Mayroyd House, when they moved in, there were nine in the family: father, mother, three girls and four boys. 'The lads got wed,' May said, 'and we lost one girl'. William Barker, the fustian manufacturer, had lived at Mayroyd before them. His manager lived in the cottages next door.

The sisters were bright as buttons, fresh-faced and extremely pleasant. They were rather like a double-act. Annie was the older by a bit over a year. She had an almost actressy manner. May was more homely, bustling about.

In one corner, a display cabinet was full of their father's poultry trophies. May brought out a big cup for Wyandotte bantams, which he won three times, and so got to keep. There was a big pile of lesser medallions, each in a little box, like a jewel box. The emblems of a long tradition. 'They're just getting to be lumber,' Annie said. 'We keep trying to get shut of them. I took one to the jeweller to get it made into a brooch. 'Sorry,' he said, 'it's only lead.' When father won first prize with a bull calf at Hebden Bridge agricultural show, the photographer came up to take the calf and the family at the same time.'

The family lived up Old Town, at first, at Carrs farm. This was close to the grandiose Victorian house, where Joshua Hoyle, the boss of Acre mill, lived. By then the house was called Burnside. It had previously been 'Stalheim', Annie told me. This must have been someone's fond memory of the Norway fjords, but it presumably sounded too Germanic in the First World War. (In London, the same anti-Germanism caused the Bechstein Hall music venue to be renamed Wigmore Hall.) The young Whitakers went to school in Old Town. 'Jonas Crabtree was the headmaster, very strict and just like a little cock robin. They were happy days.'

They went straight from school to Redman's sewing shop. 'It was no shock to start work,' Annie said. 'We knew we'd have to. We were glad we didn't have to go into Acre mill. Mother dreaded us going there. It hadn't a very good name. Some of the men and all that. At Redman's, the [sewing] machine shop manager was a grand old feller. Grandfather marched me up to him and said "Now, Annie, this is your master. Do as he tells you." We loved Charlie. We walked down from Old Town every morning.'

May went off into the kitchen. We settled down to have tea, while we kept talking.

Annie remembered her fifty-three years working at Redman's: 'I never thought to go anywhere else. Our grandfather worked there, our mother and an aunt, and four of us younger ones. At the mills there was the overpowering heat and dust. They tried to stop you talking. In the sewing shops you could talk. But at the end, I felt I'd had enough. May regretted it, though. She loves machining.' Annie said she now got as much money in her pension as she ever earned at work.

'There was a Miss Hurd at Redman's,' Annie said. 'Her invalid mother wouldn't let her marry this man she were courting. She married late but she were happy for a few years then. Miss Hurd encouraged me to read. Things like *Silas Marner* and Dickens. I found all of them dry. Some of the old books had too much padding. *Lorna Doone* was one of my favourites. I always had my nose in a book at lunchtime.

'The work was nearly all corduroy – except in the wars, when it was uniforms and duffel coats, which they called "torpedoes" then. I've never liked cord since working at Redman's. Cord stank. I would never buy a cord dress.'

Annie had 'always been a reciter. My first time was at a Band of Hope tea party. The piece I chose was entitled "Mocked".' She and May smiled at each other.

Annie said 'Mother was a real reciter. She said "Annie, no." But I said, "A few a year."' May said 'She goes all round. There used to be many concerts at chapels. Now it's mainly old people's clubs.' Annie straightened herself up in her chair, put her tea cup down, and began:

Jones was as kind, good-natured a man as you might wish to see.
He had a buxom, tidy wife and bright-eyed children three.
But Jones was weak in one respect. He had a love for rum,
And often from the drinking shop would staggering homeward come.

Fortunately for all, Jones ended up going on the wagon. 'I was encored,' Annie said.

Redman's kept going, even through the General Strike of 1926: 'The sewing shop had alternative power'. But in the worst of the slump, Annie and May were laid off. 'There was one woman we remember with kindness at the Labour Exchange, handing out the dole. But some of the officials were very cocky, thinking they had gone up in the world. Father went round Old Town, delivering the *Hebden Bridge Times*, to make a bit o' money. He said to t'driver, as I remember "Thy paper's no good." He wasn't complaining about what the paper wrote. He said "It's no good for leeting t'fire."'

We all smiled again, in the warmth of the room.

On the wall, Annie and May had a large colour picture of the Queen. 'She's our favourite lass. She's had no easy job. Edward shirked his duties and Mrs Simpson wouldn't have made a good queen. She was too domineering. She did get him, though, and at least they stuck together.'

At the Whitakers', I was in a room where everything seemed rock-solid. The certainties were all in place. I felt sorry to leave.

# 28. HENPECKED

Ernest Ainley was like a friendly tortoise. His wife, Vera, was a bit more severe. The Ainleys' house, at Nazebottom, was at a bad corner on the Hebden Bridge–Todmorden road. But at the back of the house were the quiet canal and Callis wood, with its bluebells and deer, which is the start of one track up to Stoodley Pike. We talked, in 1978, in front of a blazing coal fire.

Ernest left school at thirteen. He was twenty-one years at the Co-op shoe shop. Before that, he was at Pickles's boot shop. At the Co-op he was in sales, at Pickles's he was in making, repairing and selling. But he began at Leicester House, on Market Street, a 'smart' draper's and shoe shop (which survived until the 1980s). 'There were no clogs at Leicester House. The boss, Robert Greenwood, was conductor of the Hebden Bridge male voice choir. The hours were eight till eight. It was busiest Friday night and Saturday. On Saturday night we walked to and fro on Market Street, seeing if we could pick up a girl. The Sunday night it was down the turnpike. It wasn't pubs then.

'My father was in the cotton trade, a cotton twiner. Then he came to Callis mill to look after a pair of jinnies [spinning frames], as a master twiner. I were born in this house. My father's mother lived here, then we got it. The wife moved in next door but one, but we were already courting. We were married in 1929. My mother were living here, also, for ten years.

'My father *could* argue. I don't know where he got his knowledge. He helped start the Labour Party in Hebden Bridge. I remember those old socialists, J.R. Clynes, H.M. Hyndman, George Lansbury. When father came back from t'pub, my mother knew in a minute. His face were red. 'Politics again,' she'd say. There were two Tories who went to the pub, former Territorials, right soldiers of the Queen, you know, and we used to draw them on. We said anything that were against the country.'

Ernest and Vera loved music. 'My mother's side were a very musical family. She'd a brother who were a very good bass singer. He won a prize at a music festival in Keighley. My mother were in the Nazebottom chapel choir. My father could do a bit: he could play a tin whistle as well as anyone I knew. I met my wife in the chapel choir. I became choirmaster. There's no choir to master now. We have one festival every year now, we call it Calder Valley choir, from various churches. We'll sing Stainer's *Crucifixion*, like.

'Now I'm in an over-sixties choir. I've been there sixteen years. We're short o' tenors: are you any good? Nazebottom chapel is still open – just. The next preacher is an ex-steel worker in his forties, retraining as a minister. Percival Sowden, managing director at Moss's dyeworks, were a lay minister for many years. Now there are under twelve people in the congregation most Sundays. It used to be packed, and had an orchestra [with the emphasis on the *e*]. There was old-fashioned dancing, and we played cricket, football and Book.' What was Book? 'A bit like billets. You had a wicket at both ends and a stick. You hit the billet and ran. There's still some tackle at t'chapel.'

He said he 'were never any good at shoe repairing, but it came in handy when I were called up to the army, at forty-two. I were working in t'stores. Harry Pickles came round, as an officer – he were the son of Harold Pickles at Bridge mill, and he married Gertrude Brown – and he said "What are you doing here? You're a cobbler, aren't you?" I said "You should know. I've mended your shoes since you were a little lad."' Ernest was switched to his trade but did 'a bit o' concert party, sang a few things, did plays. Flora Robson once presented us with a prize. I were a poor soldier. I would have shot to miss, I think.'

He was a member of the famous, but also obscure, Henpecked Club. 'We always meet at churches, chapels or a pub. There's an average of twenty to twenty-five. All nice chaps, really. There's a meal and drinks. We start the meeting at half past two. New members face a severe entry-do. I oughtn't to tell you about that, really. The club medical officer has to see if you're fit or not for admission. Then there's the questioning. 'How do you know he's henpecked? Does he have a washing machine? Get it sold, get it sold.' It's taking the mickey out o' the wives. It's all humbug. No names are ever mentioned.

'We always open with a hymn. There's an argument about which – only about four to choose from. We've had all sorts of silly do's. It's international now: we've one member in Austria.'

Vera said: 'Some wives won't let them go.' Ernest said: 'Some wives have waited outside, to catch that man as soon as the meeting were finished. Once, at Blackshaw Head, a taxi came to collect a member, and his wife were in it. Martin Parr came to try to take photographs, but he were turned out. He weren't married. He were living over t'brush.' (Martin did manage to snatch one picture, though.)

How did the club begin? Ernest said 'It began at one chapel's Sunday School Mutual Improvement Society.' Vera said 'Probably about 1900.' Ernest continued 'The first event was an Easter Monday ramble. Invitations would go out, 'to the 4,000 and somethingth annual event. The first secretary were a real comic. There was always lot o'codding [deadpan joking] in the minutes. It puts a bit o' fun in it.'

The club had its regalia, in mocking imitation of the Freemasons and all the lesser self-help societies, the Oddfellows, the Buffaloes, the Foresters. 'One dish says "I serve." There's a mace and a gavel. Fresh officers are elected every year – the Guardian of the Peace, the Medical Officer, the President, the Vice-President, the Mace-Bearer, the Secretary. No Treasurer – there's nothing to pay, only for your meals.'

Through this rigmarole, Vera, smiled cheerfully. The Ainleys then took me round to see their neighbour, Levi Shepherd.

Levi had a rather military air – a Yorkshire version, I noted down, of Wilfrid Hyde White (an actor best-known now for his part in *The Third Man*). On the mantelpiece was a brass cannon Levi had made. His wife, Helena, got out their collection of photographs: the 1947 floods rising up the steps of the picture house, for example. In these floods, at Mytholmroyd, my father had to come back from work by boat.

Levi's father worked at Moss's, mixing dyes. 'He couldn't read or write, but he was good at dyeing.' Levi liked 'appreciating the past through photos'. He lent me *Hebden Bridge Times* cuttings about local history. He also showed me his father's certificate – similar to my own father's – for saving a boy from drowning in the river Calder. 'The boy were drunk.'

He was born in 1895. He said he remembered 'Mrs Pankhurst coming to help in the great 1906–9 fustian strike for better wages. Eventually all t'mills came out. There was a procession through Hebden Bridge about women's rights, and a meeting at t'Co-op Hall. A set-up called the Eaves Self-Help Manufacturers started their own weaving shed. Like any adventure like that, it's bound to fail unless there's the brains and the men to run it. The strike got bad – breaking windows, trying to set fire to mills, going to employers' houses and threatening them. It was like the Luddites, really.

'We went down as children for t'fun of it. My sisters were helping, holding banners for votes for women. What happened was that there were changes in jobs. Jacquard weaving was coming in. There were new machines and new patterns. It was taking longer to weave the cloth, so on piece rates there was less pay.'

At eleven, he started work as a half-timer in the Callis mill office, just along the road from where he lives now. He 'looked forward to the office work and the night school. But I had to go weaving at fourteen. It were more money for t'family. A weaver got twelve shillings a week, versus an office boy's three shillings. I began with two looms.' His mother, a local midwife, gave birth to thirteen children of her own, 'nine of them living'.

Levi said: 'My sister, Mary-Ann dropped dead at seventeen, turning the wringing machine. Five out of the six sons served in the First World War. I'd joined t'Territorials [like Edmund Ashworth] and were in the war from the start. Territorials were t'salvation of this country in the world war.' He served in north Russia, in the British Archangel 'relief force', during the bolshevik revolution. He came out of the army in 1919.

Before he joined up, Levi had switched jobs 'into the engineering trade'. Afterwards, he couldn't get that job back. His brother, Jim, bought an old army wagon – 'he escaped from a band-cutter job'. James Shepherd's became Hebden's biggest lorry firm, and then car dealers, which they still are. Levi, meanwhile, got a job with F&H Sutcliffe's, unloading wood. In the regular Hebden way, he soon fell out with the boss. 'I said to him "Eddie, you want to stick this job. It's elephants you want here for this money."' He went back into various engineering jobs in Halifax.

He met a girl in Blackpool and got engaged. 'I went to see her and she broke it off. She couldn't say why. I came back and I went on t'rant with my savings for nearly a week. I didn't get married, after that, till I was thirty-five. I joined t'Black and Tans – what they called the Royal Irish Constabulary – during the Sinn Fein trouble. I used to drive an armoured car. The pay were £4 12s 6d a week. It were a good job.

'I enjoyed it in a way. It was a very hectic life. You were very likely to be shot at. They dug a hole in the middle of the road, and put twigs across, to trap you. Then they'd straight away open fire. They often fired buckshot, but they might as well have fired pebble-stones at a vehicle that had quarter of an inch of armour plating. If they threw Mills bombs [a kind of hand grenade], we threw them back.

'When I came back from Ireland, it was back to dyeing. Then I became a delivery man for Co-op bread. Till I got married, I paid my mother jock brass [money for his keep]. I was twenty-five years at the Co-op. It was secure and the Co-op paid superannuation. That's been a godsend.' He switched to Mytholmroyd Co-op for his last five years. 'I'd had a wage dispute with Hebden Bridge Co-op. They were so stupid. The committee decided to knock off four shillings a week from wages. There is jealousy between working men. They talk about peace, but you have to knuckle under.

'I thought, though, that Jack was as good as his master. And I left. Down there, in Mytholmroyd, they were really gentlemen to me. The Cooperative Retail Society took over the Mytholmroyd Co-op, but not Hebden Bridge, so I got my superann. Many at Hebden didn't. There was that embezzlement business with Frederick Chatburn. But you can't just criticise *him*. At the meeting, I moved a vote to sack all the committee.

'In Hebden Bridge, not a lot of people stopped at one workplace all their lives. That were the local work position: you took what you could, learned another trade, though corduroy and dyeing were the mainstay. At the Co-op I was doing all sorts of things. I'd service wedding teas, funerals, and deliver bread at all hours and at weekends. That's why the Co-op went bust. It was *too much* of a service. At a funeral, it was boiled ham and tongue. They used to reckon that two 2lb loaves were sufficient for forty people. A quarter-pound of tea made forty cups. The you needed two Madeira cakes and a bun apiece. There's allus enough. Some of the people at a funeral are so sorrowful; others are glad to get rid.'

Levi took pride in how well he could drive lorries and vans, and 'set' engines. In the Second World War he worked at Rolls-Royce and at building submarines. That's where he made the toy cannon out of brass that sits on the mantelpiece.

He didn't resent his brother Jim's success in business. Some, he seemed to think, take risks. Others look for some security. He liked to think back to his childhood. Getting a basinful of black peas from Pea Jack, who came round with a cart and a heated pan. Going to Long Harry, the grocer, with an empty jar for 'a ha'porth o' treacle': 'My mother said "Walk in t'middle o't road, in case anyone jumps out." As childer, we'd play Whistle and Shout, where the others hide and whistle and you have to find them. Or there was Chuck 'Oil, where you'd dig a hole with your heel for the taws [marbles], and had two taws each. The first to get two in won, and the rest forfeited their taws to him.

'We weren't innocents, by a long way. I brought a clothes line from home and we tied all the doors up there open. There were about fifty children around, everyone had six or seven then. We got a jolly good cursing for that. On Mischief Night, we'd do all sorts of things. We'd tinkle windows, using a button on a thread, pulled by a string. We ran and shouted after we'd annoyed 'em. We'd put paper up downspouts, then put a match to it.'

It was a long time before all these forms of tolerated mischief died out. Growing up at Mytholmroyd, I belonged to one of the three local gangs – no one older than about twelve, no one younger than about eight. Each gang had dug a 'cave' in a field, and covered it with branches and sods. There was a chimney for a wood fire. This was the headquarters. We sat by the fire, smoking cigarettes rolled from old tea leaves.

In the long sunny evenings, it was all more like *Just William* than like turf-fighting in the Bronx. We had set-piece fights over territory. They were usually at Paddy Bridge over the railway line – named after its Irish builders – which happened neatly to divide our gang from our main rivals. But I don't remember anyone being seriously hurt. We had a bright idea one evening, with handfuls of sulphur we'd bought from the chemist's. We crept up to another gang's cave, threw the sulphur down the chimney into the fire, then blocked the hole up with sods. An interesting experiment.

In the run-up to Bonfire Night, each gang went 'progging' – collecting dead tree-branches from woods, or bringing combustible waste from workshops – for their own bonfire. You had to keep guard over it all, in case another gang stole it. The big moment was 1945 when the wartime ban on bonfires was lifted and there were three bonfires in one year: VE Day (Victory in Europe), with a dummy of Hitler; VJ Day (Victory over Japan), with a dummy of General Tojo, narrowly chosen for this honour over Emperor Hirohito; then Bonfire Night itself, with the dummy of Guy Fawkes.

On Mischief Night, we played the tricks Levi Shepherd remembered from his own childhood.

# 29. OWLS

When I first walked up to Thurrish, the last farm up the Crimsworth valley, the brother and sister, Charlie and Sarah Hannah Greenwood, lived there, and had done for many years. They opened the door pleasantly enough, but they didn't want to talk much. I was told they hardly ever spoke to anyone, though Martin Parr, helped by Susie, had been taking some very evocative photos of them. Martin may have been on his way back from Thurrish when he was photographing my family and me at Crimsworth Dean beck in 1977. He described Charlie and Sarah Hannah as 'the icon of Hebden Bridge's rather dark and gloomy, rather miserable past'. Susie saw them more positively: 'Extraordinary, eccentric, living in the most extreme discomfort and poverty, yet so open and innocent.'

Now Thurrish is farmed by Brian Hodgson and Elaine Poole. They invite me into the main room. There is a little bar at one end, laden with various items. In the rest of the room, I notice clocks and warming pans. The room is full of all kinds of objects, everywhere: unopened gifts, jigsaws, plastic bags. There are canaries in a cage. On one old beam you see the creel marks where oatcakes used to be hung.

It is hard to find a place to sit down, so we talk standing. The farm was built around AD 1600, they think, 'on the long house system: a mistle [cowshed] at that end, then a kitchen, then here, then a peat house'. As at Colden school, this means no corridors, with each room opening direct into the next. The old creel is in the peat house. 'You had to cut peat up on t'moor. It just smouldered, but that was all they had.'

Brian came here in 1979, after Charlie and Sarah Hannah left. (So I had been trying to interview the Greenwoods only twelve months before their departure.) 'Charlie would have been born here,' Brian says. Elaine joined him at Thurrish later, after she and her husband separated. Brian is heavily built, with a white beard, glasses and a woollen shirt; Elaine is smaller and more sharply dressed. 'I belonged to the same pigeon club as Trevor Poole,' Brian says. 'My own marriage wasn't working, and I clicked with Elaine. That were twenty years ago.' They have about 150 acres, they tell me, though two-thirds of these have now been reclassified as moorland. 'There's no money in farming,' Brian says. 'All they want you to do is manage the land and the wild life, leave the margins for the birds. We let all the sheep go at the end of last year. Life became so difficult. Once you could borrow from the bank but not now. In farming, you need a degree for the paperwork.' They still have forty cattle, if you include calves. 'But you can't get enough hay to feed the stock.' The land belongs to the Savile estate.

Brian and I walk out together to look at the farm. A curlew rises high over the fields, crying 'Pewit, pewit.' Guinea-fowl fly up, clattering. 'I've seen buzzards here, oystercatchers, storm cocks [mistle thrush], kites.' Brian shows me the old piggery. It is as well-built as the house. 'It used to be pigs below, hens above. Irishmen used to come each year to help out with the haymaking. They would sleep above.' He also shows me the old outdoor lavatory: 'Just a bar across, and a stream running through it.'

The canaries, chirping away in the house, came from a brood begun by Brian's father. 'He asked me to take them on. It got down to one, who then needed a mate. It went on from there.' Brian and Elaine also have a pair of barn owls: not wild, but bred. 'We were given one,' Brian says, 'and we bought the other. We go out and fly them.' At the moment, the owls are sleeping.

Below Thurrish is White Hole farm. The date over the door is 1731. On the day Charlie and Sarah Hannah politely declined to be interviewed, I came here to see Stanley Greenwood. Now he lies in the Pecket Well graveyard. But that day, he loved the chance to talk about his family. Heat spread out from the White Hole coal fire in an enamelled range. There were comfortable old seats beside the polished brass fender, books on the piano, and a spike of old bills Stanley wanted to show me. Mash for the animals was being boiled on the stove. The atmosphere was very soothing. Stanley's brother was dozing, in cloth cap and clogs. A young dog was stretched out under his chair.

Stanley and I began by talking about mutual connections and relatives. He had been pursuing family records as far away as the archives at York He gave me a copy of his list of Greenwood by-names (see page 163). The Greenwoods had been at White Hole for generations. They had continually expanded the size of their Savile estate leasehold farm as other farmers dropped out of the business. Pigs and poultry had all gone: 'We couldn't compete with the bigger firms.' What was left were sheep, cows and 'sucklers' (suckling calves). Some of the sheep were *lonks*, a very local, long-bodied breed.

Not long ago (Stanley said) there were two rent days a year, at a pub in Hebden Bridge, 'the first Tuesday after the 20th of July, and the first Tuesday after the 20th of February'. Now there were far fewer farms, and Lord Savile's agent, Preston Jones, came round to collect. 'There's been a tremendous drift from agriculture. You could get more money working in industry. The policy of governments has always been cheap food. It didn't matter if it was slave labour, so long as it was cheap.'

Stanley was a stalwart of Crimsworth chapel. 'It's a steady congregation,' he said, 'with a good attendance on special occasions'. Not any more. I go past the chapel, now a house, on my way from Pecket Well to today's White Hole farm. The farm is now run, not by Greenwoods, but by David Sunderland – though he, also, is from a long-established Crimsworth family. His wife, Anne, is the daughter of Lord Savile's head gamekeeper. We work out that her father must have managed the teams of beaters I used to go on the grouse moors with.

The Sunderlands have three children: two girls and a boy. 'But you might say the farming will end with me,' David says. 'Farming changes,' Anne says. 'Trying to make a living out of it . . . you couldn't pay people enough to do it.' The previous winter, like Kay Barret downstream, they had been snowed in – for ten days. Today they have both been up since 4.15am.

David took over the tenancy about thirty years ago. He has 300 acres or so. He won't tell me how many sheep he has: 'Sheep aren't a thing you discuss. Asking a man how many sheep he's got is like asking how much money he has in the bank.' He looks to one side, smiling. The house has been much modernised since I talked to Stanley Greenwood. The kitchen, where we talk, is prettily decorated, with blue and white plates on the dresser. But, like Brian Hodgson, David says that 'farming is not a good business to be in'. There used to be ten small farms in the valley: all have gone. 'They now go for such prices, as houses, that you could never buy one back as a farm, even if you could borrow the money.'

As I come back from White Hole farm, the hillsides are dappled by sunlight and shade. It is a landscape with fewer and fewer people in it. I think back to Thurrish and White Hole farm. People like Brian Hodgson and Elaine Poole, and David and Anne Sunderland, are like bastions of an older order. I feel privileged that they let me interrupt their lives. They embody the ghost of Hebden Bridge past, you could say, with all its virtues.

# 30. DREAMS

When I was younger, and walked the lanes below Mount Skip at dusk or night-time, I was always convinced that an upright coffin might be following me. I tried not to look. All these years later, I have no interpretation to offer for this waking dream – or nightmare.

There always seemed to be something untamed about this landscape. At 1,339 feet, Skip is the highest hill on this side of Hebden. The setting is a lot more tamed now, I'd say. This afternoon, I'm walking up the steep road to Skip in order to look at Daisy Bank: a cluster of stone-built detached houses, erected ten years ago by an outfit called Phillen Homes Ltd. I wonder whether 'Phillen' is a joke-word, meaning 'fill-in'. In the countryside, the developer's best way to get round the planning committee's doubts is to claim that your proposed new estate is only 'infill'.

The road to Daisy Bank which leads up past the Dodnaze council estate. The estate has a beautiful outlook across the valley below. The older houses are the postwar variety which were built from steel. (Somehow the government had managed to created a shortage of bricks.) I thought that such houses would never sell, but a Hebden Bridge estate agent tells me she has just sold one of the former council houses, at the edge of the estate – because of its cheapness and its view.

Daisy Bank has the same view. The names of the eight houses, set around a cul-de-sac, are a dream of rurality: Shepherds Nook, Badgers Croft, Green Royd, Broadcarr House, Meadow Bottom, The Springs, Field House, The Beeches. They read like the genteel names of sets in ITV's long-running *Midsomer Murders*, or a West Yorkshire version of it. The great appeal of *Midsomer Murders* is that it, at no point, bears any relation to real life. But Shepherds Nook and Badgers Croft stand solidly here. A dream delivered on.

They are built on the site of a mink farm. This used to be one of the ways in which subsistence farms tried to make a bit of extra money. The anti-fur protests and – for those who couldn't care less about such protests – the easier inflow of east European furs, put paid to that. The mink farm's neighbours were pleased to see it closed. The dead chickens, and such-like, that they were fed on, gave out a nauseating smell. Also, the mink regularly escaped. The tale of an elderly woman, a few fields away, was repeated with much gusto. She went to her outside lavatory in the dark, sat down and found a mink in it. 'Puss, puss,' she said, thinking it was a cat. When she realised what it was, she ran out, screaming.

It's not certain what happened to all the mink after the farm closed. One ecologist in Hebden Bridge waves his arm upstream and says, 'They're all here, in the river bank.'

The Daisy Bank houses all have double garages. Some may even have room to keep three cars out of the rain which can drive cold and hard across this hillside. Like nearly all 'executive homes' anywhere, they have very small gardens. I suppose the estate agents will chat about 'easy maintenance' – but the size is really a function of the planning system and the price of land. The result is a strange disproportion between house and site. The house doors are studded like the entrance to a castle, but they give on to tiny front patios. The windows are mullioned, which in time may give a hint of ancientness. It is remarkable how soon Hebden houses weather, even after ten years.

A grid at the entrance to the estate makes sure that no actual sheep from the hillside stray from their proper domain into, perhaps, the patio of Shepherds Nook with its artificial little stream and its metal heron.

I begin to feel like a lost sheep myself as I potter around, looking at windows and writing notes. No matter. There is no one at all at home today in Daisy Bank. This is commuter country. A nice place to come back to. Down in Hebden Bridge, Nicola Jones, chairwoman of the Calder Civic Trust, is a marketing manager with a Sheffield law firm – very pleasant, very efficient and very devoted to Hebden. She commutes daily: an hour and a half, each way.

The old streets of Hebden Bridge itself have been revivified since its old industries collapsed. But, curiously, its population hasn't grown. There is a high percentage of single people and childless couples. The terrace houses don't work well for what many people now wish for in a family home. Once children arrive, there's a drift towards Mytholmroyd, where the wider valley permits more estates of newer houses.

The other trend is embodied by Daisy Bank. If they have the cars to commute in, or alternatively if they can work from home, people drift up on to the surrounding high land. Closely enwrapped by hills, Hebden Bridge itself – dare I say it? – can sometimes feel oppressive. A sort of parody of the idea of 'community'. You could call it a kind of toy theatre. On all the local committees and campaigns, you meet the same people.

Behind the attractive sheen of arts and crafts, Hebden has become 'normalised'. It is no longer a working class place, though there are still lots of people here who are from that background. (There are also lots of workless.) The proportion of middle class is probably now much the same as in the rest of England (and the proportion of graduates is higher). Many might reject the class label, but objectively that's the case. The French, as so often, have invented a handy word: *BoBo* – meaning 'bourgeois, tending towards bohemian'. The true BoBo tends to prefer a bike to a car, and likes to live in former industrial or commercial settings. Just stand in Hebden and look around you.

Less objectively: none of this matters. Hebden couldn't have survived as an active, creative, argumentative place if it had remained the way it was. Or, to be precise, the way it had been since the great upsurge in industrial work, for both women and men, from about 1870. An upsurge which was, in fact, amazingly brief, and which wound down from the start of the twentieth century. At first so gradually that, growing up here, I was far more aware of continuity than of decline. But then the decline became precipitate. Without 'greentrification' – rural gentrification – gloom would have settled in.

'If we want things to stay as they are,' the Prince of Lampedusa wrote, 'things will have to change'. It wasn't inevitable that Hebden would be saved from the fate of so many mill towns in decline. Walking along the canal towpath from Mytholmroyd towards Hebden Bridge, you pass a strange array of narrowboats with names you could well dismiss as pretentious: Occam's Razor, Orinoco, Green Man, Passing Strangers. Luckily, names like Kanbedun, Goodwill and Bumpkin add a little healthy vulgarity, and redress the balance. So does a little painted notice on one boat: 'Hippies use back entrance. No exceptions.' But the main thing that is borne in on me as I walk is that Hebden Bridge feels like a place people care for and nurture (even if they may have rows about the exact means of caring or nurturing).

Where else could you go into the local tourist and information centre with an impossible crossword clue reverberating in your brain – 'Form of white magic practised by the early Neo-Platonists' – and be told the answer? Which is 'thanurgy'. In his spare time, the man behind the counter writes about myths and all kinds of weirdnesses

Leaving Daisy Bank, I fold up my notebook. It's starting to drizzle again. Good Hebden weather. Down a side-lane, Twine Cottages have a display of stone bed-warmers on the window sill and a Range Rover parked outside. The next house is Winter Royd. The millstone-grit houses are lovely, but the names strike a chill. I need to get warm and walk along the hill road to The Lane Ends pub. Just beyond the pub is the site of Acre mill. To re-use this old cotton mill for weaving and moulding asbestos was one way to try to claw back past prosperity. This went drastically wrong. The mill site has been cleared and grassed over. Trees were planted and a plaque unveiled. At least 250 people – mostly former workers but sometimes near-neighbours of the mill – fell victim to asbestosis, and died early.

Lane Ends proudly advertises its phalanx of real ales. On Friday nights, Indian dishes are brought in specially from an award-winning restaurant three or four miles away. For two meat curries, one vegetable curry, with rice and naan bread, the price is £7 a head. Shelves overflow with holiday paperbacks: read here, or else take away with you and pay what you wish into the charity box on the bar. But it's not all beach-type reading. I eat my steak and chips, gratefully; pick up off the shelf a worn paperback of A. Alvarez's study of suicide, *The Savage God*; and read about Ted Hughes and Sylvia Plath.

This *is* Hebden Bridge, after all.

# A NOTE ON WORDS AND PLACES

The Calder is one of the lesser known rivers of Yorkshire. This may be because it runs west–east through or beside numerous industrial or ex-industrial towns, and never enters the North Sea in its own right. It joins up with the river Aire before it gets there. In the heroic days when rivers were scoured out to take deeper boats, and the canals were dug, the outcome here was (and is) known as the Aire & Calder Navigation. Until recently the Calder valley was never classified as a 'Yorkshire Dale'. It at no point touches the Dales national park.

The Calder begins its life in the Pennines. That first stretch, down to Halifax, is the 'upper Calder valley'. This was all part of the vast medieval parish of Halifax, with no independent churches or chapels of its own. Now it is all rolled up into the hyperbolically named 'metropolitan borough of Calderdale'. This operates from Halifax town hall, and is little loved in the higher reaches of the Calder.

Halifax itself lies above the valley, on a small tributary of the Calder called the Hebble. Other small towns and villages sprang up at various tributary points. A run-down village called Luddenden Foot – where drunken Bramwell Brontë briefly held down a job in the long-gone railway station – is an easterly outlier of the 'Hebden' I am writing about. This is where the tiny Luddenden brook tipples down into the Calder, passing the pre-railway hamlet of Luddenden on the way.

Hebden Bridge is where the Calder is joined by the Hebden river. The junction point is called Black Pit, because the Rochdale canal passes over the river here and cuts off all sunlight. Throughout the upper valley, in fact, the Calder lurks in the background, like a wallflower at a dance. The canal and the railway are much more obvious markers in the landscape.

Hebden Bridge, narrowly defined, is a fairly small place. The village of Heptonstall – much older than Hebden Bridge – lies above, on a craggy promontory, three sides of which are marked off by the Hebden, Colden and Calder rivers. The flat land behind the promontory is called Heptonstall Slack (a 'slack' was where a hill evened out). This gives rise to always-entertaining names for the two ends of the hamlet which sprang up on this easier land: Slack Top and Slack Bottom.

To the east of Hebden Bridge lies Mytholmroyd. Before Calderdale borough was invented in 1974, the two villages had for many years been jointly administered under the title, Hebden Royd. Now they form the Hebden Royd civil parish. Mytholmroyd is where the Turvin brook, otherwise known as the Elphin brook, runs into the Calder. The side-valley itself is always known as Cragg Vale, and there is a tiny hamlet at its mid-point, also called Cragg.

Going westward, the next settlement upstream from Hebden Bridge is Todmorden. This is technically in Yorkshire but it is always perceived as a Lancashire-style cotton town (even though Mons mill, a gigantic redbrick landmark, has been demolished). At one time the Lancashire–Yorkshire county boundary ran bang through the middle of Todmorden. The postal district is 'Lancashire', and the postcode, OL, links it to Oldham. Todmorden has the residues of its heyday as a genuine town, especially its magnificent town hall.

Hebden Bridge and Mytholmroyd are surrounded by the upland parishes of Heptonstall, Wadsworth, Erringden and Blackshaw, with their many scattered hamlets. Before the railway came, and tugged manufacture down into the valley, these hamlets were the heartland: small-scale farming plus the spinning and weaving of local wool.

In all the uplands you are never far from a dam, created by a Hebden manufacturer to feed his mill, or a reservoir – sometimes created by the old canal owners to balance the water level of their canal; more often created by the Halifax water board to feed the long-dead demands of Halifax's own industries. Many dams have been emptied out because people had a tendency to drown in them, either accidentally or deliberately. The reservoirs look as though they'll be there till Kingdom come. Hills and water: these are the hallmarks of this millstone-grit landscape.

Hardcastle Crags, the woods owned by the National Trust, lie on the upper reaches of the river Hebden.

I use 'Hebden' as the simplest way to describe everywhere, hill, stream or valley, between Todmorden and Luddenden Foot (but not including either). I apologise to any friends, relatives or other local patriots that this may offend, but I can't think of any simple designation which would be any better.

---

About pronunciation. If, like me, you are a reader who likes to know how words are pronounced, even if you are reading without moving your lips, a few remarks may help. The BBC almost always gets these local names wrong, even though so many media people now live in Hebden and could tell them better.

*Todmorden* has the stress on the first syllable: TOD-mor-den, not Tod-MOR-den. The *mor* and *den* both have that blurred vowel sound, *er*, represented by lexicographers with an inverted e. You get this bargain-basement vowel at the tail-end of many English words. (Locally the place is usually called 'Tod'.)

*Heptonstall* was always HEP-on-stal, with the same blurred vowel for *on* and *stal*. (And the H would usually be dropped.) But this short form has gone the same way as many other English place names (for example, *Sisister*, as the way to say Cirencester, is more or less dead). Pronunciation has moved closer to the spelling. So you now often get HEP-ton-stall, with only *ton* hanging on to the blurred vowel, and *stall* pronounced like 'market stall'.

*Hebden* is usually HEB-din, among people born there; and often without the H. Newcomers seem to prefer HEB-den, with *den* sporting the omnipresent blurred vowel.

*Mytholmroyd* is the biggest trap, it seems. Hardly any outsider ever gets it right. Given that Ted Hughes was born here, which means that the name crops up semi-regularly, this is surprising. Even the BBC's latest pronunciation guide doesn't set producers right. The correct pronunciation is MY-thum-royd, with *my* pronounced as in 'my town' and *thum* pronounced like *thumb*, but with a hard *th*, as in *this*. Practice makes perfect.

I hope this helps. . . . In older local speech, Mytholmroyd became, simply, *t'Royd*, and Hebden Bridge became *t'Brig* (with a hard *g*). The inhabitants were Royders and Briggers.

———————

This is probably the place to talk about the Yorkshire *t'*. Bear with me, because this, also, is so often got wrong. Before a consonant it is *not* pronounced as a separate letter. It is simply a sign for a 'glottal stop' – the kind of swallowing sound that Cockneys and speakers of Estuary English also insert instead of *t*: as in *be'er* (for *better*) or *ma'er* (for *matter*). One reason why Yorkshire speakers are supposed to be better at learning German is that they already know all about the glottal stop (with which German is bespattered) and pronounce their northern vowels as pure sounds, not southern-style diphthongs. Before a vowel, the *t'* is pronounced or else expanded to *th*.

But let's not go into all that. In this book, I have seldom tried to transcribe full-on Yorkshire. But I have sometimes used hints of it to give a flavour of how some people I quote do, or did, speak. Full-on Yorkshire is a dialect (like Lowland Scots, or Lallans), not merely an accent. But, for years – decades even – this ancient English language has been retreating to hilltops and backwaters, and has almost died out. RIP.

# ACKNOWLEDGMENTS

My deepest thanks go to all the people in Hebden Bridge, Mytholmroyd, Heptonstall and the surrounding hillsides who, at different times, agreed to be interviewed by me. Not everyone appears in this book by name, but what I've written is imbued, throughout, with what I learnt by listening.

I was, at various stages, encouraged in writing this book by three historians, Asa Briggs, Raphael Samuel and Colin Ward. I draw on two academic studies direct: PJ Higham, 'Social and economic regeneration of declining industrial communities: a case study of Hebden Bridge', D.Phil. thesis, Council for National Academic Awards/Manchester Polytechnic (now Manchester Metropolitan University), 1986; and Darren P. Smith, 'Rural gatekeepers and 'greentrified' Pennine rurality: opening and closing the access gates' (*Journal of Social and Cultural Geography*, vol 3, pp 447–63, 2002). I have also drawn on the files of the *Hebden Bridge Times*, the *Halifax Courier* and the Hebden Web.

The lines from the poem 'Dick Straightup' are copyright by the Ted Hughes estate and are reprinted by permission. An earlier version of Edmund Ashworth's story was published in *Prospect* magazine.

I am very grateful to Richard Hollis for his careful reading of the MS, at a point when I thought it was fine, but it wasn't quite. I also thank all those – especially my sister Elaine – who so willingly helped me with information and checking. For help on the illustrations I thank Martin Parr, Daniel Meadows, Frank Woolrych, curator of the Alice Longstaff Collection, Chris Radcliff, Andrew Kim and Philippa Lewis.

Last but not least, I express my lasting gratitude to my family and friends, who gave me a reason for writing this book.

*Paul Barker*
*January 2012*

## PICTURE CREDITS

Frontispiece: Andy Hawkins; Map : Ordnance Survey. Plate 1: Elaine Pullin and author; Plate 2: Colin Billingham, Alice Longstaff Collection, Birchcliffe Centre, Hebden Bridge; Plate 3: Author; Plates 4, 5, 6: Alice Longstaff Collection; Plate 7: Author; Plate 8: Author, courtesy of Veronica Plowden; Plate 9: Martin Parr and author; Plate 10: Martin Parr; Plates 11, 12: Hebden Bridge Handmade Parade – Queen Bee on bridge, puppet by Alison Duddle, photo Nigel Hillier; Veronica the dragon, puppet by Thingumajig Theatre, photo Craig Shaw; Plates 13, 14 : Mike Barrett, frogsdesign; Plate 15: Hebden Bridge Little Theatre; Plate 16: Daniel Meadows; Plate 17: Alice Longstaff Collection; Plate 18: Eric Williams, courtesy of Chris Ratcliffe, Pennine Pens; Plate 19: Martin Parr; Plate 20: Fay Godwin; Endpapers: Bedrock Geology UK South, British Geological Survey, 2007.

# INDEX